For all the fat girls who have spent their whole lives feeling invisible. I see you.

Also for Jason Momoa. You're a really great guy, but you're married, so I think we should just be friends.

Fattily
Ever After

Stephanie Yeboah

Hardie Grant

BOOKS

Contents

Chapter ONE

Body Positivity?

OK...BUT GIVE BLACK WOMXN BACK THEIR THINGS

DISCLAIMER ALERT!

This book for me is, first and foremost, a love letter to fat, black womxn. For womxn who look like me, who have had to grow up navigating spaces where we have been made to feel unwelcome, judged, and sidelined. I'll be talking about a lot of topics that some may see as sensitive or 'cutting', so to speak.

Alongside this love letter, and as well as including my own personal experiences and anecdotes to highlight specific topics, I also include ideologies and statements regarding – for the most part – white womxn, slimmer womxn, and the power plays and structures that have been enforced throughout history that have been instrumental in the oppression of not only ethnic minorities, but bodies that – in society's view – would be considered not to have any privilege.

When I talk about slim privilege or white privilege in this book, I'm talking about these privileges at a *societal/sociological* level, as opposed to a personal level. These privileges mean that you may not be exposed to fatphobia, body policing, racism, racial microaggressions, prejudice, and other overt and subtle injustices due to your skin colour and body shape. The privileges have absolutely nothing to do with how you personally feel about yourself, or your circumstances. Understood? *Wunderbar!*

However, if you're the type to have your feelings hurt by the truth, whether it be my truth or truths that fellow plus-size womxn and black womxn share as our realities, take this as a disclaimer: this book isn't here to coddle the feelings of white womxn or womxn with bodies that are deemed as socially acceptable by society. In order for change and growth, accountability must be taken. And while we can blame most things on cishet, white, middle class men and the patriarchy in general *shakes fist*, it's also important to talk about how white womxn and white feminism have been implicit in silencing less-privileged bodies within the body positivity movement. You have been warned!

'The truth is, body positivity is for white womxn. White female bodies being safe is paramount to upholding white supremacy.'

– Me, 2017

The table is shooketh!

I bet you're asking yourself, 'Ahhh – did Steph actually have the unmitigated gall to quote herself at the beginning of her book?' The answer is yes. Why? Because it's MY book frankly, and I gets to do what I want. Isn't it wonderful?

Within these pages, you'll get to read all about me and my thoughts on navigating life as a black, plus-size womxn in the UK. I'm about to tell it as it really is, without any holding back.

Some of you may know me already, as I've been out in these online streets for the best part of 11 years talking shit and looking slick, but if you have no idea who I am and have just bought this book on Amazon because it showed up in the 'books you may like' panel alongside a plethora of other non-fiction books written by other British and 'body positive' influencers, then let me introduce myself: my name is Steph and I'm a British, fat, black womxn with a lot of thoughts and feelings about *stuff*. By *stuff*, I mean topics including intersectional feminism, inclusivity and diversity within the media and EVERYDAY LIFE, fashion, topless Jason Momoa content, and most of all, being fat and all the fuckery that comes with it from society.

Growing up as a black, fat girl in the UK can be quite traumatic to say the least, I'll tell you that for free. We went *through* it back in the day, didn't we? The fat jokes, the 'you're so blick' jokes, invisibility, the colourism, the rampant fatphobia, the mockery – we went through it *all*, and even though we are currently in the throes of this so-called 'Body Positivity Revolution', plus-size, black womxn are still losing out and being marginalized in favour of our socially acceptable, whiter counterparts. It's about time we had our views and perspectives listened to, don't you think?

I grew up in a moderately suburban part of south-west London, to two Ghanaian parents who had lived in the UK for some time. My dad, whilst being born in the UK, spent his childhood and early teenage life in Ghana. My mum, born in Ghana, spent the majority of her child and teenage life in south-east London and Kent, with the latter making her the only black child in her primary and secondary schools.

My dad attended boarding school in Ghana, where bullying and hazing were seen more as rites of passage than anything else, which is why he always had a somewhat 'meh' attitude towards me getting bullied in school, from what I can remember.

My mum on the other hand, went through the kind of outlandish racism that a lot of us today would only see on TV. From being caught up in the BMP riots in her local neighbourhood, to being bullied for being black at school, my mum pretty much lived through it all, which was the reason for her 'no nonsense, I've-had-it-worse-than-you-at-school' approach when it came to my struggles and issues with bullying.

Primary school was a breeze for me. I hadn't yet encountered the feelings of insecurity and low self-esteem in regards to my weight, even though I was a bit chubbier than the other kids. After spending two years of schooling in Ghana, being caned by Catholic nuns for merely breathing, running around the sugar cane fields and eating nothing but plant-based foods for the duration of my stay there, I came back to the UK to see out the rest of my primary school education looking a bit smaller, but not really being aware of my body or how different it was to everyone else's at the time.

'Puberty with a side of crippling insecurity please!'

If I could sum up my entire secondary school experience using one song, it would be 'Creep' by Radiohead.

Whew! As soon as I hit 11, puberty came out of nowhere and hit me square in the face with a bag of pennies. During this period, my mum would be abroad on business for several months during the year and my dad – the archetypal African patriarch of the family – had absolutely no idea how to handle this sudden onslaught of pubescent teen angst and emotion and kinda left me to my own devices. This meant me not having any idea of how bras worked until the age of around 13, despite me being around a C cup at the time. Dressing like a tomboy did little to help with the situation either, as I tried as much as possible not to focus on what was going on with my ever-expanding body and instead, found ways to cover it up with a host of tragic fabrics and coveralls. A kind of 'out of sight, out of mind' situation, you know?

I remember first being bullied on my first day of secondary school, due to my 'weird sounding' surname, which by the way, I absolutely loved and was proud of – mostly because people kept thinking I was related to famous-at-the-time Leeds football player, Tony Yeboah.

From that, the insults about my weight began. I was bullied for being dark skinned. Bullied for being overweight. The verbal insults quickly turned into physical acts of violence against me and because I was the quiet one in school, I refused to talk about the bullying to anyone.

I remember even going so far as to sign up to help out at my school's breakfast club which started at 7:30 am, because I wanted to avoid the bullies on the way to school. Proper NERD qualities right there. My duties included making breakfast for the kids who were dropped off to school early. On the days when it wasn't as busy, I'd help myself to several bowls of Sugar Puffs, Coco Pops, and devour slices of toast, laden with butter. Excessive eating became my way of dealing with the bullying and the more I ate, the bigger I became which in turn led to the increase in bullying. It was a constant circle of woe.

I remember being in the communal changing rooms

during PE and noticing that my body was drastically different from the other girls; their boobs were plump and perky and were decorated with pretty, frilly bras from Tammy and Per Una at M&S. I, on the other hand, had these triangular mounds of droopy, stretchmarked flesh that pointed downwards towards my rounded belly. The other girls would have gorgeously cornrowed, wavy hair complete with delicate swirls of baby hair expertly slicked down to frame the perimeters of their faces. I, meanwhile, had to make do with wearing bandanas over my hair every day to cover up my thick, damaged hair that bore the brunt of my mum's Jherri Cur! (otherwise known as a curly perm, in which strong chemicals are used to create curls that are semi-permanent) experimentation.

My mum being absent during puberty, really did make things hard when it came to basic things such as doing my hair, finding bras to wear, and general teen maintenance. I began distancing myself from the others at school as I didn't feel like I fitted in with the standard of beauty that had already been set. I wasn't light skinned or mixed race, therefore I was bullied for it. I didn't have wavy, manageable hair and I wasn't slim. I was being beaten up and verbally abused for existing and, when the time came when I did happen to mention the bullying at school, I was told verbatim that I should perhaps 'lose weight so they wouldn't bully me as much'. That was the day I internalized my self-hate and blamed myself for existing in the body I was born into. Fun times, right?

That was the day I began to actively hate myself. I was 12 years old.

School was the absolute worst if I'm being honest. If you're reading this and you knew me from school, just know that I absolutely hated it, regardless of the face and attitude I presented to the public on a day-to-day basis. Hardly anyone intervened when I would get picked on at school, and this further cemented my belief that maybe the bullying I was receiving was deserved. From having acid thrown at the back of my neck in science class, to being choked and nearly losing consciousness outside our classroom before French class began, I'd see the faces of all my peers in the background, just looking on and either laughing, or saying nothing at all. It was then that I decided to completely shut down and internalize my feelings. I did end up seeing the lovely school counsellor, whose son I had THE absolute biggest crush on BTW (whew), and I would scatter some thoughts and emotions every now and again, but aside from that, the foundations of the bubbling pit of depression that I would eventually be diagnosed with two years later were beginning to take form.

One crowning moment in my bullying experience I will always remember, was during what was I believed to be an 'invigorating and insightful' Sociology class. In all honesty, I'd always hated that class as it contained two of the six or seven boys who made my life a living hell. I would normally sit at the back of the class in a bid to not be noticed or seen – the usual – but on this occasion, our teacher must have been running late by about 15 minutes or so (honestly, didn't they know I was in impending kinda-sorta severe peril? Sort it out!).

One of the bullies started with the usual jibes and taunts and as usual, I tried to ignore it as much as possible and get on with preparing for the lesson. He didn't like this at all, so he left the classroom in a huff. 'I'm saved!' I thought to myself. Small victories when you ignore bullies and all that. Except he came back about four minutes later carrying a huge 4'5" empty wheelie bin, which he then proceeded to throw on top of me.

I could hear the shocked gasps of the girls around me, and the whooping and cries of excitement from the boys and in that moment, I felt like utter trash (pun absolutely intended). The act was then followed by taunts and jibes such as 'no one's gonna like you', 'you're butters' (ugly), 'you fucking fat bitch', and 'just kill yourself because your life is already over, fatty'.

It's funny isn't it? How sometimes it's not the physical pain that leaves a lasting impact, but the emotional and psychological pain. I remember the event as if it happened only yesterday, and while I have worked through that specific trauma of my life, it's still something that isn't easily forgotten. That night, I went home and started cutting into my tummy with scissors, in a bid to 'cut' it off. I was an absolute mess.

The exclusion I felt didn't just stop at school, oh no. I'd go home, turn on the TV and see images that made me further dislike the body I was born into. In the early 2000s, we barely had enough black, British television shows, let alone black, fat characters, so I found myself tuning into Trouble TV and MTV Base every day to watch the latest American sitcoms, aching to find someone I could relate to – someone who looked like me.

It almost didn't seem fair that America at the time had so many amazing black-centred TV shows, whilst all we had in Britain essentially was *The Real McCoy*, *Three Non-Blondes* and *Little Miss Jocelyn*.

I ached for shows that would highlight fat, black womxn in a positive light. At the time, I needed to feel validated, and I looked for representation that could show me that it was okay to look the way I did, and that I could be fat and still be confident, fabulous, and outgoing, but alas. From being teased at school, constantly comparing our bodies and appearances to lighter-skinned girls, to the media invisibility, skin bleaching, and dieting, being fat and black always felt like somewhat of a burden. It's like society regarded us as being bottom of the barrel.

That was until a little movement called body positivity began gaining prominence online in the late Noughties. A movement which was to change the game forever.

OK let's get this straight once and for all: WHO 'created' body positivity?

Ah! The age-old question. The question that spawns a plethora of Twitter thinkpieces and shady indirect Instagram captions. It's important that the foundations of the movement are known and understood in order for the movement to progress in a more intersectional, fair, and inclusive way.

The body positive movement originated with the fat acceptance movement of the Sixties, which aimed to combat anti-fat discrimination and to celebrate and inspire the validity and acceptance of fat bodies. In the US, this resulted in the creation of the National Association to Advance Fat Acceptance (NAAFA), a charity organisation dedicated to combating size discrimination across all races. The organisation was originally founded by Jewish feminists, Sara Fishman and Judy Freespirit, who had come out of the Radical Therapy Movement and wanted to install more radical ideas surrounding the way society

'I ached
for shows
that would
highlight fat,
black womxn
in a positive
light.'

saw fat people and more specifically, dieting. When told by the organisation that their messaging was 'too feminist' *rolls eyes*, they quit and subsequently formed the Fat Underground Movement, and went on to create the now legendary Fat Manifesto in 1978, which I implore you all to Google and have a good, long read, because it's absolutely excellent and will have you 'YASSSSSSS!'ing until the cows come home, frankly.

The movement – as well as the general ideology of 'body positivity' – experienced a quiet period throughout the Seventies to the early Noughties, as we entered the era of the 'Supermodel', in which we saw the likes of pioneering models such as Kate Moss, Naomi Campbell, Christy Turlington, Linda Evangelista, et al, spearhead the 'waif chic' and 'hyperfeminine' trend that was rampant throughout the Nineties.

The movement then experienced a resurgence in the late Noughties, as an increasing number of black and non-white, plus-size users, bloggers, and activists began to use online social platforms such as Tumblr, Livejournal, Yahoo! Messageboards, and Blackplanet to create safe online mini communities for fat womxn to celebrate and appreciate their bodies without fear of judgement. These communities were accessible via the use of the #FatAcceptance hashtag, which then later graduated to the #BodyPositivity hashtag as some fat womxn were still (and are still) a bit unsure about self-identifying as 'fat'.

These up-and-coming communities provided us with a forum to discuss the complexities of marginalization, and to celebrate diversity in all its forms, whether that be physical, sexual, or racial.

I discovered the body positivity community back in 2012 after creating a weightloss-tracking Tumblr account. At the time, it was still a somewhat diverse community celebrating self-love and radical self-acceptance of fat bodies of all races. But this inclusion was a given, seeing as the re-emergence of this important movement stemmed from predominantly black and Jewish plus-size womxn in the US.

Every night after work, I'd come home and immediately track the food that I'd eaten for the day onto my Tumblr account that was followed by absolutely NO ONE. Because of the types of food and weightloss-heavy posts I was engaging in, I guess the algorithm started showing me all blogs that had anything to do with bodies, and so it became such, that while scrolling through my main feed to look for the latest fitspo 'before and after' post, I'd have to scroll through huge amounts of self-love and self-appreciation posts by fat womxn. As time went on, I began to spend more time looking at the fat acceptance posts, and less time submitting my weightloss stats.

One Tumblr user in particular caught my eye. Her name was Tati-ana Brissett, but she went by the name 'Marfmellow' online. I instantly became utterly obsessed with this absolute Queen. She was shaped exactly the same as me, but where I severely lacked the confidence and self-esteem, Tati-ana thrived in it. She dressed exceptionally well, she was funny, absolutely stunning, but most of all, she was 100 per cent unapologetic and this moved me. I began spending more time on her page, scanning the online stores to see where I could buy an outfit she had been promoting that day. I became obsessed with wanting to have the amount of confidence she had, and to this day I count her as one of the womxn who really inspired me to undertake the journey towards self-love.

Suddenly, Tumblr no longer became a chore for me. No longer did I log in to expose myself to the dangerous dieting habits I had been abiding by forever. I started unfollowing all the dieting accounts that had made me feel terrible over the years and started following the accounts featuring bodies that looked like mine. I stopped following the weight-trackers, anti-fat quote pages, and 'inspirational body' meme pages, and started following pages featuring stretchmarks, hyperpigmentation, rolls, and cellulite.

Tumblr was no longer a warzone where I had constant battles with my body. It became a fat paradise of sorts; a heavy haven – a squidgy safeplace featuring a plump plethora of bodies that looked like mine. I suddenly felt less alone, and began to reach out to these womxn to ask them about their journeys towards self-love and self-acceptance. I needed to know their secrets. How did they muster up the courage to...go out in the summer without wearing cardigans and other clothing items that hid their so-called flaws? How were they able to take full-length photos of themselves without becoming repulsed at their image? How were they able to convince themselves that they were worthy of love, while looking the way they did?

I had so many questions. So many queries. SO many places to go in this new-found movement! And so, like my heroine *Dora the Explorer*, I packed up my backpack which was filled to the brim with the tools that I hoped would lead me through the rocky terrain of self-love, and I set off on my way.

Self Loooooove

Body Positivity:

1960s
Fat Acceptance/liberation started gaining popularity with the creation of the NAAFA by predominantly Jewish and black womxn.

1970s–1990s
'Thin is in'. Athletic, lithe frames were all the rage and dominated the media as well as societal aesthetic standards for the best part of 30–35 years.

Early 2000s
Hip Hop video vixens arrive on the scene, marking a slight change from the 'thin' status quo that audiences had come to associate with beauty. These models (who were mostly African American and Latina) were known for their big breasts, small waists, and large bums and thighs. Albeit a small departure from the norm, a departure that eventually didn't go unnoticed nonetheless.

2007
Kim Kardashian's sex tape is leaked online. The public is exposed to seeing a white womxn with 'curves'. The world becomes obsessed with her hourglass shape.

2008–2012
The rise of the Tumblr Fat Acceptance generation. Fat womxn of colour take to popular journal online platform Tumblr, to flood the websites with photos and affirmations of self-love and body acceptance. Content consisting of everything from poems to cartoons to photographs depicting larger fat womxn become all the rage and it is on this platform that a lot of content creators and influencers start their body positive journey, by using the hashtag #bodypositivity.

A Timeline

2012–2016   Larger plus-size bloggers and influencers worldwide begin to make huge waves within the fashion and lifestyle industries. There is a resurgence in heritage plus-size brands who are looking to update their 'dated/middle-aged' aesthetic to fit in with the modern, confident, and edgy pieces of the late Noughties.

2015–today   Mainstream fashion brands begin to take notice of the online popularity of plus-size bloggers and content creators. Noticing their tendencies to go viral and make headlines, brands start to create plus-size collections and extend their mainstream collections to include larger bodies. A profitable decision.

2016–today   The media begin to take an interest in the hottest new 'trend': self-love and body positivity. They begin to write articles and feature body positivity spokesmodels who are predominantly white, slim or hourglass shaped, and conventionally attractive, while simultaneously leaving non-white and larger fat people feeling a bit lost within the community.

Today–today   A schism develops, with the radical fat acceptance crew on one side, and the #"AllBodiesMatter"BodyPositivityCrew on the other. Other offshoots of the positivity community begin to develop, such as Skin Positivity and Hair Positivity. Today, body positivity is a movement with its own standards of beauty – which is normally white and white passing, hourglass/pear shaped or smaller, a big bum and high cheekbones.

Some black influencers and activists of note who have helped shape the body positivity movement

Gabi Gregg

Founder of Gabifresh.com, plus-size swimwear and lingerie designer and co-owner of plus-size label, PREMME.

Describing herself as the 'OG Fat Girl', Gabi Gregg is a well-known American plus-size writer who started her blog, 'Gabifresh', in 2008. Gabi went viral in 2010 after posting a series of photos of herself wearing bikinis on social media platforms such as Instagram and is widely credited for coining the popular term 'fatkini'. Gabi continuously advocates for more variety and quality within the clothing market for all shapes and sizes and has designed several plus-size collections with swimwear brand SwimsuitsForAll, as well as collaborating with lingerie brand Playful Promises to create several collections of her own plus-size lingerie.

Hunter Shackelford

Visual artist, cultural journalist, and director of Free Figure Revolution.

Hunter Shackelford is a prominent cultural writer whose work focuses on popular culture, identity politics, blackness, and fatness, and has been creating content on these subjects via her social media platforms since 2013. Her cultural essays and socio political commentaries have been featured in publications such as *Wear Your Voice Magazine, Buzzfeed, The Washington Post,* and *The Feminist Wire.* As a content creator, Hunter also curates information to create tangible sources for vulnerable communities in addition to programming and creating safe spaces for marginalized bodies.

Hunter is also the creator and director of Free Figure Revolution, a southern body liberation organisation that empowers black, fat, queer, and trans bodies through community initiatives and programming.

Jessamyn Stanley

Yoga instructor, writer, and body positivity advocate.

Jessamyn is a plus-size yoga instructor, writer, and body positivity advocate based in North Carolina, US, whose classes provide a body positive approach to yoga which aims to celebrate students' bodies and encourages them to ask 'How do I feel?' as opposed to 'How do I look?' when practising yoga.

Jessamyn started out journalling her daily yoga routines on Tumblr, where she slowly began to amass an audience of people who also wanted to get into yoga but were too conscious about their bodies to do so. She has released a body positive book entitled *Every Body Yoga* which gives an uplifting approach to yoga and teaches how to weave the practice seamlessly into your daily routine.

Tati-ana Brissett

Known as Marfmellow online and a key figure in the plus-size community since 2009.

Through the use of social media platform, Tumblr, and her YouTube channel, Tati-ana A.K.A. Marfmellow has been a prominent plus-size activist/influencer who uses her videos and blogs to talk about a host of different subject matters within the plus-size community. From plus-size fashion reviews and dating tips, to showcasing her curves via beautiful imagery on Tumblr, Tati-ana has inspired a host of plus-size womxn to fall in love with their bodies, and has helped others on their journeys to achieving self-confidence.

'Before I found tumblr, I never really saw fat black femme representation outside of TV show *The Parkers*. I was in love with HAES (Health at Every Size) and radical fat acceptance because I grew up being told all the time that my body wasn't worth showing off or feeling good about. I can't say I would be where I was without those movements because they truly was the catalyst to me learning about autonomy and consent as well as the theory that fatphobia derives from antiblackness.

We are living in a world that doesn't see value outside of privilege, so the fat black womxn is damn near erased and yet we are hyper visible as fuck throughout history as mules and mammies. Because of those facts, I feel my body is by default political, and depending on who is in the room I oscillate between not being seen or being seen for all the wrong reasons.'

– Tati-ana Brissett (Marfmellow)

In recent years, however, the movement has become a lot more commodified. Body positivity is now a 'free-for-all' movement monetized and politicized by brands and public figures, in ways that often result in individuals above a certain size and darker than a certain complexion, being left out of the conversation.

As body positivity became more mainstream, I noticed that the conversations were also most often centred around white womxn. Arguably, much like the feminist movement, we are now at a point where body positivity has become non-intersectional and tends to constantly prioritize the thoughts, feelings, opinions, and achievements of white womxn, with a small number of 'token' non-white womxn being sprinkled throughout campaigns like parsley, in their 'look at us being diverse!' quota.

It seems that the present movement lacks direction and focus, and prioritizes the thoughts, perspectives, and visibility of white, able-bodied, cisgender womxn with hourglass-shaped or smaller bodies (womxn who, let's not forget, already fall well within society's acceptable standards of beauty).

Slimmer, white people (womxn) can love themselves loudly, quietly, or not at all, but they will almost always be seen as 'normal' in the eyes of society at large, regardless of if they feel normal in themselves or not. They will likely not experience overt or covert discrimination based on their size; neither will they face ongoing pressure to lose weight in order to be accepted.

When people talk about body positivity in this way, they are looking at it from the perspectives of themselves as individuals. They want to feel confident about the way they look (who doesn't?), and they find it hurtful to be told that the body positive movement wasn't designed to support them.

But this is not, or at least should not be, an #AllBodiesMatter situation. Of course, all bodies are equally important, and I hope that everyone reading this – whether they are a size 4 or a size 30 – feels good about themselves. But body positivity is not about boosting the confidence of people with conventionally attractive and 'acceptable' figures. It's not about logging onto Instagram and seeing a barrage of attractive, white, thin (or thin adjacent) womxn bending over as HARD as possible to create a smidgen of a micro-roll in order to prove to their thousands of followers that they too (!!) are 'normal, real, womxn'. We know you're normal – society knows you're normal – and you are constantly treated as such!

The world affords certain privileges to people whose bodies fit within the standards of beauty that society dictates we have, in order to be seen as 'normal'. By dismissing the movement by citing 'all bodies matter', it glosses over the abuse, marginalization, and 'othering' of unprivileged bodies that fall outside the scope of what is seen as 'beautiful'.

Instead, it is a social movement aimed at removing the prejudices that make us value some bodies more than others. It is incredibly political, something that should not be overlooked or forgotten. And like feminism, any approach to body positivity that refuses to acknowledge hierarchies of privilege – that refuses to learn from those who are more oppressed, and that neglects to fight for those more marginalized – is missing something crucial.

Why is body positivity important for black womxn?

Simply answered, because the black female body (in all its shapes) has been dehumanized, mammified, hypersexualized, and fetishized since the days of slavery, by the patriarchy and by white society. If our bodies weren't being used for comedic relief in comedies and cartoons, then they were being used as cautionary tales.

Allow me to throw in a bit of history if I may.

There has been a lot that has been written about surrounding the aesthetic standards for womxn during the Renaissance. Back then, to be larger and plumper was considered to be the 'ideal', but it wasn't just about the size of the womxn's bodies. The standards would also take into account body shape. A proportional and well-rounded body was all the rage back then, and as the population of black womxn who came to Europe as a part of the slave trade increased, the more these beauty ideals of having the 'perfect larger' shape were cemented in the countries that benefitted most from the slave trade. Coincidence? I think not.

The population of African womxn as slaves and domestic servants in Northern and Western Europe between around 1490 and 1590[1] frequently led to the incorporation of black womxn into the lexicon of what was defined as the 'perfect female body' at the time. The inclusion of black womxn as beautiful in both fine art and aesthetic discourse wasn't without its problems.

African womxn were described as well-proportioned and curvy, and consequently viewed as physically appealing, yet the discourse about Africans suggested that their distinctive facial features made them facially unattractive. Adding to that their servant-status, black womxn at the time were further denigrated. Despite their reputation as 'well-formed beauties', their African faces and slave status set them apart from their high-status European counterparts.

This would continue for hundreds of years, and eventually would cause Italian and French scholars to take it upon themselves to examine the black, female body. 'Why is it that the black, plump body is deemed as desirable? There must be something wrong or alien involved, therefore we must study them, TBH'. Definitely paraphrasing there, but I'd like to think that that was running through their heads when they decided to prod, poke, and dissect the bodies of black womxn, in the name of 'research'.

A hugely popular example of this is the tragic tale of Sara Baartman. The tale of Sara is one that myself and other black womxn have heard growing up, told to us by family members or lightly spoken about during Black History Month. However as I got older, I began to do more research online on Sara and her tragic life, and what it meant for other black womxn like her living through an era where black womxn were seen – and treated – as less than human. There are many articles and biographies of Sara online, should you wish to find out more about her, but here I thought it would be good to give a condensed version of her story.

Sara was a South African womxn from the Khoikhoi tribe, who lived in the 1770s. The womxn of the Khoikhoi tribe were best known for their elongated labias and large bums, and because of this, Sara was taken from

1   https://www.liverpoolmuseums.org.uk/ism/slavery/europe/black_
    people.aspx

her homeland to England and France, where she was first used as an exotic dancer for sexual entertainment within the military.

From there, she was whisked away to England to be exhibited like an animal within a variety of freak shows until her death. Audiences would come from far and wide to see Sara and her 'freakish' curves. They would touch and prod at her vulva (for an extra fee of course) and laugh and gaze in wonder at the size of her bum. Her figure was deemed different from the feminine standards of London at the time.

Sara was seen as both grotesque and exotic: a hypersexualized specimen with a peculiar racial identity. An absolute pisstake if you ask me. After her death in 1815, her body would continue to fascinate scholars for many years to come. Her body was given over to science, and her vagina was excavated, studied, and put on display in France until it was returned back to South Africa in 2002.

The presence of Sara Baartman in Europe, and others of her tribe, was an important factor in the reinvention of the so-called 'Hottentot' (an offensive term the Europeans called womxn from the Khoikhoi tribe) and how they were viewed by European society. Their presence as a symbol of black femininity helped make fatness an intrinsically black, and implicitly off-putting form of feminine embodiment in the European scientific societal imagination. You absolutely hate to see it!

Some Patriarchal Westernized Standards of Beauty
A CHECKLIST

- ☑ White
- ☑ Slim
- ☑ Athletic
- ☑ Small nose
- ☑ High cheekbones (where available)
- ☑ Clear skin
- ☑ Tanned (but not too tanned, otherwise it's labelled as trashy =/)
- ☑ Able bodied
- ☑ Proportioned body type
- ☑ Long hair
- ☑ Long legs
- ☑ Practically perfect in every way

The marginalization of black womxn/WOC in campaigns and movements

While it's important to acknowledge and appreciate brands that feature plus-size womxn, I can't help but notice the lack of models of ethnically non-white backgrounds, who are constantly being left out or side-lined in favour of their caucasian counterparts. It is very easy to spot the common theme in these campaigns; white, with high cheekbones, and an hourglass shape. It's not just the fashion industry, either, oh no! There are multiple examples of white bodies which fall outside of beauty standards being revered, while fat womxn of colour who are of a similar size and body type are ridiculed, tokenised, or ignored altogether.

American lingerie retailer, Aerie, released their ongoing '#AerieReal campaign in early 2014 in a bid to promote body positivity through their use of un-retouched images in their marketing materials. While the campaigns every year have been somewhat diverse, a large percentage of the womxn they choose are white, with only one plus-size black womxn being included for the 2018 run of the campaign. Similarly, a 'body positive' campaign created by Victoria's Secret in 2014 entitled 'The Perfect Body' induced outrage when the marketing images were released which found that not only were the majority of models white, but all of the models were very slim, too.

US plus-size retailer Lane Bryant, responded to the Victoria's Secret campaign with a body positive campaign of their own called #ImNoAngel. The movement was created to empower all womxn to love their bodies, however, it was another campaign which eventually fell short due to the tokenism of placing one lighter-skinned, hourglass-shaped, black womxn among a group of white womxn, which was noticed on social media.

Skincare giant, Dove, has also garnished criticism online for their #RealBeauty campaigns which typically featured small or hourglass-shaped white or light-skinned womxn, often omitting fat, black womxn altogether, although now through various global influencer campaigns, they are working to become a lot more size and race-inclusive in their messaging and advertising, which is always a great thing to hear. I could go on and on about all the well-intentioned-but-ultimately-failed body positive campaigns built on the backs of black womxn, but you catch my drift, right?

Actually nope, let me touch on one more. The most popular body positivity trope.

You're scrolling down Instagram minding your fat business, and then suddenly you're shown images of mostly thin, white womxn, flaunting their *ever-so-slightly* curvy thighs with cellulite or posing cheekily in a bikini, eating pizza, gripping the one roll of fat they managed to form, all in the name of 'LIBERATION!'.

The truth is, body positivity is for white womxn. Accordingly, white female feminists who claim to be here for all womxn, play favourites with whose bodies they covet and uphold, and whose body-shaming is worth reviling. While people within the body positivity community have to deal with gender equality and size equality, black womxn have to deal with the above, as well as race equality and colourism. Which makes it even more imperative to include all bodies, regardless of colour, and to give a voice to those who are not represented fairly.

Here's hoping that one day in the future, the community and those outside of the body positive movement, will see us as a collective and not marginalize within a group that is already in itself, pretty marginalized. There are so many different experiences, opinions, thoughts, and perspectives, and everyone deserves to be heard and represented, not just the thoughts and experiences of those with privilege.

Which is why I'm writing this book, because our perspectives need to be told and shared. Black womxn matter. Fat womxn matter. Black, fat womxn matter. It's important that the body positivity movement includes, engages with, and better understands the experiences of fat, black womxn, to ensure it becomes a truly inclusive movement that breaks beauty standards in all its forms.

Ideally, one of the first places where we need to see that shift happen is within the media.

How to be an Ally

So, you've made it to the end of the chapter: congrats!

If you're black or a person of colour, you will have probably recognized a lot of the issues I touched upon in the intro chapter and are ready to move on to the next one. If you're white and/or non-fat, I bet you're probably now wondering ways in which you can be a better ally to black womxn and womxn of colour within this movement right? Riiiiight????

Well fret no more, as I have some tips below on how you can achieve better allyship and to help uplift those who brought this wonderful movement to the forefront.

First of all, let's talk about some things black womxn and womxn of colour want from allyship:

'Respect us'

'Speak up'

'Listen to us'

'Talk to other white people'

'Don't take over'

'Stand by our side'

'Don't assume you know what's best for us'

'Don't make assumptions'

'Find out about us'

'Understanding'

'Don't take it personally'

Know that allyship is a relationship

Being an ally is a continuous relationship. It's hard, OK? It has its ebbs and flows and you're going to go through good times and bad times. There will be times when you will have to apologize continuously and probably vice versa. Being an ally is not like writing a CV, you cannot just build up a list of things you've done and wave it around in class like Hermione Granger on steroids. You don't get a badge that you can pin onto your jacket and shine up so people notice it. It shouldn't be performative. Once you become an ally, you've got to know the person or people you want to align with, and they've got to know you too. You have to build trust, and with that comes patience.

Learn how to hold other white people accountable

Becoming accountable starts with a question: what is accountability? *The Oxford Dictionary* defines it as 'being held responsible for your actions'[2]. When we talk about accountability in this case, it means holding yourself responsible for the privilege you possess as a white person or as a smaller-bodied person. Do you tend to talk over non-white people during discussions about body positivity? Do you make generalized comments about the movement without thinking about the womxn who helped pave the way for it to progress? Do you often 'like' or repost 'progressive' body positive campaigns which only seem to feature white womxn?

Holding others accountable can mean going out of your way to talk about the ways in which an individual or a brand has treated a group of people, either by total exclusion or tokenism. It means speaking out about unfairness and calling for actions for change.

It also means intersectionality: if you call yourself a feminist/body positivity supporter, your feminism should encompass the struggles of black womxn and womxn of colour, and should not just be 'white feminism'. If you are talking about body positivity, you should be including the rights of black womxn and womxn of colour in your dialogue, and should not be using whiteness as a normalized baseline.

Listen

This is a good strategy for any situation. You will not always be an expert in everything. If there is someone who knows more about a particular topic within the body positive space, or has more lived-experience or less privilege than you (either by being non-white or a larger fat person), *listen to them* and do not try to downplay their experiences. You shouldn't be talking over those with experiences of low-to-no privilege, fatphobia, or racism – value others' thoughts and contribute your own in a way that is additive to other's experiences, not reductive of them.

Recognize that the body positivity movement = fat acceptance movement

The body positivity movement stems from the original fat acceptance movement that was made popular by larger fat womxn and womxn of colour. This fat acceptance movement, must exclusively look, sound and feel like fat bodies and experiences, as those are the only bodies that can encapsulate all of the nuances that lie within this specific marginalized community. When smaller womxn take up space in body acceptance movements by centering conversations on their own experiences, they inherently push out more vital voices. Instead, smaller-bodied womxn should talk with each other about their own internalized fatphobia and the ways they contribute to the systemic oppression of fat womxn. Thin womxn can be supportive of fat womxn, but only when they're careful about how they show up and unpack their own (albeit often unintentional) oppressive behaviour.

How to Involve Yourself Within the Community

40

So, you've decided that today will be the first day of the rest of your life. You want to change your mindset around how you think about, and view your body. You want to surround yourself with like-minded individuals, and wrap yourself up in a cosy little safe space where you can celebrate your body, and engage with content featuring the thoughts, opinions, and perspectives from people who look like you. Yay!

You log online, however, and see that the community that you once saw as being 'inclusive' is filled to the brim with white, slim, cisgendered, socially acceptable fat, or slim-looking womxn. WHAT TO DO? Well, there are a couple of spaces online where you can thrive and be made to feel welcome and included.

If it's literature and theory you're looking for...

I feel like this book would be a pretty good start?
I mean I hope that the information found within these pages go some way to providing a broader context to body positivity and black radical fat acceptance, as well as discussing themes and experiences that only we can really identify with. I mean I don't wish to BLOW MY OWN HORN or anything but you know...picking up this book is one of many great decisions you'd be making!

Wear Your Voice Magazine. www.wearyourvoicemag.com
A feminist magazine that provides a plethora of intersectional body positivity hot takes, essays, theories, and perspectives. Created, edited, and written by a talented group of womxn of colour, this online publication will give you the tools of knowledge to get you started.

***Hunger* by Roxane Gay.** One of the rawest, most heartbreaking, and powerful books I've read in a decade, *Hunger* is an intimate memoir which talks about the author's journey through eating disorders, existing at the intersections of being not only fat but black, and the struggles that can come alongside that. Roxane manages to articulate the struggles and thoughts a lot of us have had regarding our body issues – an absolutely incredible piece of writing.

If you're looking for an online (or offline) safe space full of people who look like you...

Meetups! Hear me out. Now I've used meetup.co.uk (or .com!) a couple of times in the past to meet new people and it's honestly been great. While there are some meetup groups that focus purely on the fetishistic aspect of being a plus-size, black person, there are quite a few groups one can join that focus on being a safe space where people can come together to chat about their experiences navigating society, fashion, clothing, and relationships, all over a lovely meal or a few drinks!

Instagram Hashtags (but specific spaces only).
We all know that Instagram can sometimes be a cesspit of fuckery at the best of times, but for me, it was an instrumental part of my self-love development. The important thing about navigating Instagram as a fat person is to make sure that you are able to curate your feed so that you only see images that make you feel good about yourself. Some hashtags you could use could be: #fatacceptance #bigbeautifulblackgirls #tcfstyle #andigetdressed #dopecurvyladyalert #dopeblackqueens #PlusSizeWOC and #plus_isamust as a great starting point for safe spaces that feature predominantly plus-size womxn of colour. You can also use the general hashtags such as #psblogger #radicalfatacceptance for an increased reach.

Content Creators! OH HAI THERE. IT ME AGAIN. But seriously, following my favourite plus-size content creators really helped me form my own identity surrounding my fatness. Amazing content creators on Instagram such as **@ashleighthechubbybunny** (whose entire IG feed consists of predominantly plus-size womxn of colour), OG plus-size blogger **@Gabifresh**, British plus-size models **@enamasiama**, **@Curvegirlmannequin** and **@CurvyCampbell** as well as YouTuber **@ChanelAmbrose** have all been instrumental in me appreciating and celebrating my body as being worthy of love, care, and appreciation, as well as being able to share my views in a safe space of people who could understand the various nuances to being fat and non-white.

Chapter TWO

Black, Fat Womxn Are More Than Your Sassys And Mammies

'...And the Academy Award for best actress in a supporting role goes to...*Hattie McDaniel*!'

From this event, the newspapers would later describe the scene at the Coconut Grove Restaurant within the Ambassador Hotel in Los Angeles, where the plus-size, black womxn strode up the segregated ballroom to collect her award.

'*If you had seen her face when she walked up to the platform and took the gold trophy*' gossip columnist Louella Parsons wrote, '*you would have had the choke in your voice that all of us had when Hattie, hair trimmed with gardenias, face alight, and dress up to the Queen's taste, accepted the honor in one of the finest speeches ever given on the Academy floor.*'

What a time to be alive, huh? It was 1940 when history was made, as 44-year-old Hattie McDaniel became not only the first black person to be nominated and actually win an Oscar, but the first black, fat womxn in the history of Hollywood to claim the prestigious accolade. Amazing! Life changing! Trailblazing! Epic! A mood! Neverminding the fact that Miss Hattie had to eventually accept her Oscar from a segregated section of the awards' venue...swings and roundabouts innit?

McDaniel, whose parents were former slaves, was a songwriter, singer, and former washroom attendant who went on to play mostly domestic roles for the rest of her acting career. Having won the role of Mammy by showing up to the audition wearing an authentic maid's uniform (we love a Method actor!), Hattie set the archetypal tone for the specific type of submissive role that fat, black womxn would be expected to play for years to come.

For those who are unaware of what a 'Mammy' is, it's basically a predominantly southern US-based stereotype of a black womxn who worked with a white family and typically nursed the family's children. The Mammy figure is very firmly rooted in the history of slavery within the United States.

Hattie winning the Oscar for her role as Mammy the maid in *Gone with the Wind* was no doubt a tremendous feat in what was still a racially hostile era, and in her acceptance speech, Hattie said *'I sincerely hope I shall always be a credit to my race and to the motion picture industry'* which she indeed was. Soon after winning her Oscar, Hattie then went on to play predominantly domestic roles throughout the rest of her career (with 74 out of 94 roles she played in her lifetime being domestic roles[3]) saying, *'I'd rather play a maid than be a maid.'* This was met with loud criticism from the black community at

3   https://www.imdb.com/name/nm0567408/

the time, citing that her role in playing the house help was contributing to set black people back hundreds of years.

While I can understand Hattie's view that she'd rather have steadily paying work on the 'silver screen' than work as a domestic servant, they had a point. The stereotypical trope of the 'matriarchal, aggressive, loud, sassy, black Mammy' character stayed in the minds of Hollywood executives for years to come.

When I think about the roles that black, plus-size womxn in the media played when I was growing up, a lot of them – to be completely honest – were quite damaging and seemed to play on the exaggerated 'Mammy' character. Let's think about it for a second: there was always the sassy, black, churchgoing mother; the sassy, black, comedic mother; the sassy, black, alcoholic mother; the maid; and the sassy, black friend.

It even became so bad that men started playing us!!! Some popular examples include Madea (played by Tyler Perry), Rasputia (played by Eddie Murphy), and Big Momma (played by Martin Lawrence). Not gonna lie, I used to love me some *Big Momma's House* back in the day. I felt so SEEN, LMAO.

I absolutely ached for representation on screen growing up. Don't get me wrong, we were thrown scraps every now and again, with the odd fat sideline character on an episode of *Eastenders* or the admittedly amazing, yet short-running sketch show that was *Three Non-Blondes*, but if I had seen someone on screen who looked like me without all of the stereotypes forced upon them, I definitely would have grown up feeling a little less insecure about my body, and a little less alone.

When I was young, I was obsessed with Missy Elliott, which is one of the main reasons I started getting into dancing as a child. Using both music and visuals, Missy Elliott had a way of subverting the male gaze and rejecting the gender norms as a black, plus-size female rapper. The choreography in her innovative videos made me think I could keep up with her, and a lot of the time, I actually could! I started attending after-school breakdancing classes and even though I was being bullied at school during the 9–4, after school was when I really felt I could shine, regardless of the fact that I was the only plus-size person in the class. Eventually,

49

'I absolutely ached for representation on screen growing up.'

I ended up dislocating my knees after failing to warm-up in one session and that was the end of that dream but NEVERTHELESS, the spirit of Missy Elliott kept me strong, sane, and free during those lessons. She was a plus-size womxn who achieved incredible career success, commanded the respect of her peers, and thrived with this abundance of self-love inside the already sexist media and entertainment industries.

But I feel as if Missy Elliott was the exception. An amazing, rare American exception, gift-wrapped for my 12-year-old self. What I failed to see were fat womxn with wonderful sex lives and revelling in the male gaze that I had grown up always believing was important. I just didn't see a lot of confident, fat womxn who were *loved*. They were definitely portrayed as being the nurturers and giving love, but being the recipient of love? Barely saw it.

Instead, I was exposed to Weight Watchers adverts, Dawn French in baggy clothes, the perpetual pursuit of weight loss, and no indication that fatness was anything other than a flaw.

So many years of research have shown that the images black womxn see on the big and small screen affect how they believe they should look. Growing up, I longed to see myself represented on screen; didn't we all? So, when I came home from school one day and turned the TV on to my favourite channel and saw a mother-daughter combo sitcom entitled, *The Parkers*, my life was forever changed in that one moment.

The Parkers – a sitcom that aired in the States from 1999 to 2004 and was eventually brought to the UK via syndication – starred the highly acclaimed, plus-size comedian Mo'Nique as the 'man-hungry, sassy, neck-rolling mother', Nikki Parker, and Countess Vaughn as her on-screen daughter, Kim Parker. The show centred around the lives of the vivacious mother/daughter combo as they navigated the highs and lows of attending the same university together, and the embarrassing – yet fun – mishaps Kim goes through having her mother as her sudden class- and roommate.

Watching US comedic legend, Mo'Nique, portray a confident (and sexually confident), hilarious black mother on *The Parkers* did something to me. It was the first time I had ever seen someone who was shaped like me on television, without the character being portrayed as aggressive or subservient. Mo'Nique was vulnerable. She was funny, kind, relatable, secure in her body, mischievous, and had an insatiable appetite for her long-time crush, Professor Oglevee, which often landed her and her on-screen daughter Kim, in all sorts of trouble.

As well as Missy Elliot, Mo'Nique was a pivotal figure in my ongoing relationship with my body. I looked to her in a way, for guidance. I'd see Mo'Nique on her comedy stand-up tours wearing bodycon leopard print dresses and beg my mum to take me to Tammy Girl on the off-chance that they may somehow stock plus-size clothes for my frame. I'd see Missy Elliott cutting shapes on the dancefloor with the hottest routines of the Nineties and try to emulate her.

These womxn, these two black, fat womxn were instrumental in my self-growth and in me recognizing that I didn't have to limit my abilities because of what I looked like. We're now in the 2020s, and we still have a long way to go with the way in which black, plus-size womxn are represented within the media, especially within the UK.

Black men and their roles in perpetuating the black, fat womxn stereotype in media

In a now notorious scene from Eddie Murphy's 2007 film *Norbit*, a voluptuous, fat, black womxn decked out in a pink bikini has such a huge girth that the lifeguard can't tell if she is wearing bikini bottoms because her fat rolls block the view.

Madea, who stars in a series of Tyler Perry's hit movies, including the 2009 film *I Can Do Bad All by Myself,* is a large, black womxn with a sassy, buxom figure who dishes out advice – and arse whoopings. As a male comedian, Tyler Perry was offering a problematic representation of plus-size, black womxn to the masses. And this representation did not start or end with Madea.

Big Momma is a large, busty, no-nonsense, sassy 'grandmother' in her 60s who takes up a position as a housekeeper and nanny to two troublesome children, where hilarity and high jinks eventually ensue.

These images – and others like them – perpetuate the aforementioned 'Mammy stereotype'. The Mammy is usually a grossly overweight, large-breasted womxn who is desexualized, maternal, and non-threatening to white people but who may be aggressive toward men and children[4]. The most common iteration of the Mammy stereotype adds a twist, however. In *Norbit*, the Madea movies, and Martin Lawrence's *Big Momma* films, the Mammy characters are played by men dressed as womxn, adding another layer of rubbish to the desexualising stereotype. Tyler Perry's Madea almost resembles an updated 'Aunt Jemima' and is the latest in a series of portrayals by men to depict the fattest, ugliest, black womxn that Hollywood makeup artists can conjure. In addition to Lawrence and Murphy, big names such as Jamie Foxx, Chris Rock, and Marlon and Shawn Wayans have all achieved mainstream success by portraying womxn.

These films have created a culture war of sorts, as on the one hand, the Afro-Caribbean and African American audiences believe that these sorts of movies reinforce the negative stereotypes of fat, black womxn, but on the other hand, we are still spending our hard-earned money at the cinema to watch these movies! *cue Oprah Winfrey 'WHAT IS THE TRUTH?!' GIF*.

The truth is that caricatures of black womxn from men are, a lot of the time, more harmful to womxn. They constantly rely on tropes about black womxn being uncivilized, ghetto, and unattractive; stereotypes that black womxn still have to fight against every single day – and this trend hasn't changed. Even on Instagram, black comedians use black womxn as characters so much that it's not uncommon for them to be hired to promote products such as weaves, waist trainers, or harmful dieting foods.

In the movie and entertainment industry, black womxn are often villainized or caricatured unless they fall into an *extreeeeemely* narrow window of desirability. When you add in the size element, the result is a dehumanizing performance of disgust, shame, and malice towards fat, black womxn. Men have relegated plus-size, black womxn to punchlines in a way that has a real effect on how the rest of our communities view us.

53

---

4   Fuller, 2001; Hudson, 1998; Jewell, 1993

You only have to look at the way American plus-size actress, Gabourey Sidibe, has been publicly disrespected time and time again – American radio DJ, Howard Stern, once called Sidibe 'the most enormous fat, black chick' he's ever seen – as opposed to someone like Rebel Wilson, who is frequently celebrated as being the 'quirky, fun, chubby' girl and who, in several interviews, has stated that she deliberately gained weight in order to further her career. It seems that Wilson is the more appropriate canvas on which to change the world's perception of fat womxn. A dark-skinned black womxn who oozes confidence in the face of constant online bullying, isn't.

In the States, Queen Latifah is a LEGEND and Mo'Nique is hailed as one of the female comedy greats. Gabourey Sidibe has starred in *Precious*, *American Horror Story*, and *Empire*. They have Natasha Rothwell, who plays 'sassy best friend, Kelly' in HBO's *Insecure*, and Academy Award-winning actress, Octavia Spencer, who has starred in movies such as *The Help*, *Hidden Figures,* and *The Shape of Water*.

In the United States, they have countless black, plus-size personalities currently featuring both within reality TV and the small screen. Who do we in the United Kingdom have? Well, with the exception of Alison Hammond who works as an entertainment correspondent on daily breakfast show *This Morning*, Grime rapper and presenter Big Narstie, and Chizzy Akudolu who stars on medical soap opera *Holby City*, I'm hard-pressed to think of any black, plus-size people we have on our television screens. Granted, the US actresses above are playing roles that may be deemed by some as 'problematic', but the point stands that when it comes to the visibility of black, fat womxn, the United States have beat us to the punch.

In November 2018, Australian actress Rebel Wilson decided to go on a blocking bender on Twitter, specifically blocking black womxn, causing a string of controversy and backlash online. Why, you may wonder? In a bid to promote her movie *Isn't It Romantic?* – a romantic comedy about romantic comedies – Rebel decided to shake the table by proclaiming that she was the first plus-size womxn to be featured in a romantic comedy – ever.

Of course, this triggered bucketloads of backlash from predominantly black audiences online (myself included, TBH) who went on to school Rebel about the dozens of black actresses who had featured in or had starring roles in romantic comedies. Wilson further stated that the roles these black actresses had, were considered 'grey areas' in Hollywood. The absolute caucasity of it all.

Wilson's tweet ignored the several black womxn who have starred in romantic comedies, like Queen Latifah and Mo'Nique. Some of us have all seen *Last Holiday*, *Just Wright*, *Beauty Shop,* and all the episodes of Nineties US sitcom, *Living Single* episodes, in which Queen Latifah, as Khadijah James, was the object of affection for men like Morris Chestnut, Cress Williams, and Bumper Robinson. She's BEEN there and done that.

Mo'Nique again has also already been there. One of her funnier and sweeter movies was called *Phat Girlz*, and the entire premise was a larger womxn looking for love.

None of these movies were straight to video. Even if Rebel Wilson hadn't watched them, she should know about them, so why she would make the statement she did is anyone's guess – but she did.

Comments about the constant erasure of black, fat womxn within Hollywood began to circulate on Twitter. Instead of releasing an iOS Notes press release with an apology, as so many celebrities who mess up on Twitter do, Wilson's response was to double down even further and block her critics. She blocked so many people that the hashtag #RebelWilsonBlockedMe[5] became a trending topic for over 24 hours. It was a tremendous example in further silencing, sidelining, and marginalizing the very voices who are already at a disadvantage when it comes to representation in Hollywood. Rebel eventually apologized but by then, the damage had already been done.

Regardless of how many leaps and bounds Hollywood claims to have made with diversity, black, fat womxn are still an afterthought. We aren't allowed to perform femininity like our smaller counterparts can. We cannot be the unproblematic lead characters in movies, and are instead, assigned as the sassy, supportive, maternal best friend who 'could have so much potential', but is left with little-to-no character development or arc (see Kelly in *Insecure*). Even the first *Sex and the City* movie got in on the act, casting a pre-weightloss Jennifer

---

5   https://twitter.com/search?q=%23RebelWilsonBlockedMe&src=tyah

Hudson as Louise, Carrie Bradshaw's 'personal assistant', who gives her a lot of 'you go get yours, girl!' advice, delivered in that classic sassy, black womxn tone. We cannot be sexual beings! We cannot be successful, independent womxn who are secure in our bodies!

In May 2019, Octavia Spencer starred in the psychological thriller movie *Ma*, in which she played a womxn who had become obsessed with a group of high school children in a small town, leading to disastrous results. Before the release of the movie, I remember feeling excited and happy that a plus-size, black womxn would be starring as the lead character in a horror/thriller movie – for the first time ever! No sass! No neck rolling! Just a character full of pure evil – I was WAITING for this moment!

After watching the movie, however, I was dismayed to find that, *SPOILER ALERT*, the character had developed her evil streak due to experiencing trauma as a child at the hands of other school children who teased her about her size and looks. I mean...sure, this is how a lot of female villains start out. We can't 'just' be evil for evil's sake like men can – our evil has to have found its roots in men *eyeroll*, but STILL! I was pretty underwhelmed that the studio still had to make her physical appearance a reason for her personality disorder. Even fat, black, evil womxn can't just be evil without it being traced back to their size.

Take Gabourey Sidibe's role as Becky on FOX's hit TV show *Empire*, for example. Becky is a successful A&R executive who works for one of the most powerful record companies in America. She is stylish, sophisticated, opinionated, and hardworking. In Season 2, she has a boyfriend who is much smaller than her, and in one pivotal scene, they make love.

I remember watching that scene at home and jumping up and down and 'YASSSSSSS'ing with every fibre of my being, because it was the first time in living memory that I had ever seen a love scene featuring a plus-size womxn, let alone a black, plus-size womxn. The backlash on social media the next day was heartbreaking to witness in real time.

'That was disgusting as AF. Don't nobody wanna see that mess', 'She needs to lose some weight before she ends up crushing that guy', and 'That scene made me feel sick. I didn't need to see her looking like that', were just some of the comments I came across on Twitter, and my heart wept for Sidibe.

What was even more powerful, however, was the comment Sidibe hit the fat-shamers back with, in the aftermath of that episode. 'I felt sexy and beautiful and I felt like I was doing a good job...I'm not sure how anyone could hate on love, but that's okay.'

Game, set, match.

This my friends, is what we need more of on our screens. I want to see black, fat womxn getting butt-naked on camera. I want to see black, fat womxn on my British screen playing characters with successful careers, falling in love, having families, and having our own stories to tell.

Our stories are more than a witty 15-second comeback or a snap of the neck. We are more than just reaction GIFS. Our stories deserve to be told thoroughly and delicately. Fat, black womxn are dynamic. We're smart, driven and confident. We deserve so much better than the role as the invisible sidekick, or the girl who only has lines when she's worried about her figure. Portraying groups of people as monolithic (or not portraying them at all) is how anti-blackness in the form of tropes and stereotypes are upheld. We need to do better. The British media need to do better. As do the American media. Hell, EVERYONE needs to do better. We deserve it.

'I want to see black, fat womxn getting butt-naked on camera. I want to see black, fat womxn on my British screen playing characters with successful careers, falling in love, having families, and having our own stories to tell.'

The Four Most Common Stereotypical Character Tropes We See on TV

The 'Black Mama' Fat Character

The dominant matriarch of the family – Domineering. Sassy. Emotionally strong. The Black Mama loves her family dearly yet isn't afraid to shell out the tough love when needed. She isn't afraid to speak her mind, and is for the most part, portrayed as super maternal and desexualizsed. She is also often placed alongside a husband who is super submissive and a bit more tolerant of her huge personality. See: *The Nutty Professor, Big Momma's House, Madea's Family Reunion* – Almost Every Single Black Movie!

Oh no she didn't!

The 'Sassy Best Friend' Fat Character

Typically, a darker-skinned, fat womxn with barely any backstory or character arc of her own, the Sassy Best Friend is there to provide the service of an emotional crutch, and funny sidekick duties to the protagonist. The character is usually the funny character with tons of attitude and loads more extroverted than the main character. The Sassy Best Friend is confrontational and isn't afraid to throw her weight around, so to speak. She's all 'YASSSSS GURL!' and – it kills me to say it but – 'OH NO SHE DIDN'T!' See: *The Proud Family*, *Shrill*, Most Netflix teen dramas, *Insecure*.

The 'All My Life I've Had to Fight' Fat Character
This character has gone through STRUGGLES in her life, and everyone knows it. She has struggled with her weight for years and it is one of her biggest insecurities. They are shy, awkward, and generally have low self-esteem. Cut to the protagonist being the source of their ego booster, letting them know they are beautiful and valued. See: *Why Did I Get Married?*, *The Colour Purple*, *Precious*.

The 'Hypersexual TSA Agent' Fat Character

This can also extend beyond working at airport security and also intertwines with the 'Sassy Best Friend' trope. This was a trope I first noticed being played by Mo'Nique in the critically acclaimed movie, *Soul Plane*. In this movie, Mo'Nique plays the lazy, sex-obsessed security agent who never fails to mention her sexual conquests and can be seen being overtly sexual to the male flight passengers during the movie. In *Insecure*, Natasha Rothwell plays Kelly, the 'sassy' hypersexual friend of the protaganist who often goes out of her way to demonstrate how sex-obsessed she is.

Fat, Black Representation: Getting More of What We Deserve on Screen

In the era of body positivity, my Instagram feed is fat girls loving who they are and proudly hashtagging the ever popular #EffYourBeautyStandards in solidarity. But the representation on television still leaves a lot to be desired. Seeing as a lot of the top decision-making for roles lands far outside the scope of the average person like you and I, here are some tips that can help facilitate our needs and wants, to the powers that be (*spoiler*: a lot of it involves social media).

Hop onto Twitter

Twitter has fast become one of the most powerful social media tools online, and has been instrumental in getting people together, whether it's to fight a social justice cause, collectively laugh at the latest meme, or groan in disgust at the latest Tweetstorm by President Toupee Fiasco. Twitter has a knack for making issues go viral. Hop onto Twitter, find the accounts for the casting director/showrunners/ producers/directors of your favourite show and tweet them directly about your concerns of the diversity in characters on said show. Because of how quickly Twitter can become news, with the right amount of tweets from a collective of people, you could end up receiving a response from a member of the show and your hashtag could – if organized properly – turn into the next hashtag. Case in point? The #OscarsSoWhite hashtag which was started by Twitter user, April Reign, in 2015, in a campaign to get the Academy Awards to look at the lack of diversity during the awards.

Be the change you want to see (if you're talented)

Can you act? Sing? Do you have a knack for presenting? Whatever the talent you have may be, do not let it stop you from venturing out into the entertainment business. It can be difficult starting out when your entire physical identity seems to go against the grain of what showbusiness dictates, but you have to remember that sometimes if you want something badly enough, we have to be the change we want to see in society. Persistence is key. Rejection is normal. It's all a part of the process of showbusiness, but if you're relentlessly trying and you feel as if you are getting nowhere...

...Then upload your content onto social media

Social media is the latest and most innovative way of getting noticed these days. From the now-defunct Vine app to Instagram and even TikTok, the newest crop of actors, singers, and entertainers are being discovered online. Upload your creative content on YouTube and other social media channels. Share the links on Twitter and encourage your friends and family to share your content. With the lightning-pace way in which videos rack up views on Twitter, you'll never know who could be watching your work!

Encourage the fat, black creatives in your life

We all know how difficult it can be to 'break' into showbusiness – and what a ruthless business it is! But if someone in your life has that creative knack, then it's up to you to help nurture that talent, and to fill them with the encouragement they need in order to start on the path to fulfilling their dreams. Using body positive, encouraging affirmations are incredibly helpful – phrases such as *'it's about time XXX show had a plus-size lead!'*, or *'I think you'd be an amazing addition to this song'* can really help someone's self-esteem and see them apply for that casting. You never know!

Create Your Dream Fat Protagonist Challenge

If you could create your ideal fat protagonist in say, a movie or TV show, what would that look like to you? How would they be navigating society in their fat bodies? Would they be a comedic character? A villain? The 'Monica-from-Friends'-type neurotic friend? I find that there is so much power in not only saying things out loud, but speaking things into existence, even if it means jotting some ideas down and having a think about the types of representation you want and DESERVE to see on screen!

For me, I have always wanted to see a fat, black version of Carrie Bradshaw, but not as problematic. She'd be in her early 30s, a successful, confident creative who is super intelligent, super witty, and just living her best life, as well as being in a successful, loving relationship, as I think it's mega important to show that fat people can be shown as being in relationships that don't focus on one of the parties feeling insecure or suffering from low self-esteem. Self-love is incredibly important, and it's important to own one's sexuality and learn how to fall in love with yourself every day. Self-love and self-appreciation are the cornerstones of positive body image, as well as helping to set the foundations for any future relationships one may have, however, it's also equally important that we as plus-size womxn and black can be shown as loveable, sexual, desirable creatures who are happy in themselves, and in their bodies too!

What would your character's name be?

Age? Career?

What is their origin story?

Where would they live?

What would their personality be like?

What genre of TV show (or movie) would they be a part of?

How would they dress? Would they be popular?

Successful? Rich? What's their story?

Chapter
THREE

Navigating The Cesspit Of Fuckery That Is... Dating!

'She's FAT!
NO thanks.'

– Lewis*[6], Year 4

'I think you're cool,
but I'm not into fat girls.'

– Nathan*, Year 13

'Sorry, Steph,
I guess I just
prefer her body shape.'

– James*, 2nd Year of Uni

'She's taller
and has a
more hourglass
shape.'

– Ex

'You look
like a bit
of a saucy minx!
I've never tried
chocolate before.'

– Most men on
dating apps

'...Can I be your slave?
I want you to dominate me.
You look so aggressive
and I want you to fu-...'

– Again, most men on dating apps

'......no.'

– Men in general

*All names have been changed to protect the identities of those
mentioned (like fuckboys need more protection, LMAO iKid iKid).

💔

I mean...where to even bloody begin?! In a nutshell – speaking from my own experiences – it's absolutely shit basically. I was single throughout the entirety of my teenage and early adult life, and it suuuucked. Sure, a part of it was probably due to my crippling insecurity about how I looked and my general introvertness, but a large part of it was due to my size.

A plague on both your houses Sebastian* & Lewis*...a PLAGUE!

I remember the first ever crush I ever had: I was in year two and his name was Sebastian* (*ahemfakenamecough*). Sebastian* was – put simply – an angel sent to this earth to live among us mere mortals. He was Colombian, and had the most beautiful coffee-coloured, smooth skin. He had thick, wavy dark hair that flopped over his incredibly huge, hypnotising, foggy grey, hooded eyes. I mean, me remembering every fine detail probably says an awful lot about how in LUST with him I was, considering I haven't seen him since finishing primary school in 2000. Sebastian* was a vision, and all the girls in our year had a thing for him. I remember trying to come up with ways to get to know him, but to no avail. Before I knew it, however, I was snatched away to live in Ghana and would not see him until my return to London almost two years later. At that age, I didn't really understand the concept of heartbreak as my attraction towards him was purely physical, but I remember writing his name over and over again in my textbooks in school, thinking about the day when we would finally reunite, and I could tell him what was in my heart.

Luckily enough for me, once I came back to London I was sent back to the same primary school and as chance would have it, we ended up in the same form group!

I WAS REUNITED WITH SEBASTIAN*. This was going to be the start of something serendipitous and beautiful! *cue angelic choir singing in the background and Cherubs flying above*

Please ask me if this guy even acknowledged my existence...pls?! By then, we were in year four and he had grown a bit taller and was looking 'even more' amazing. After constant attempts to try and talk to him, he absolutely palmed me off by telling me to lose weight before I spoke to him.

I was nine years old.

Let's now cut to year five, when I developed a new crush (because #ByeSebastian*!).

Lewis* was his name. I decided that this time, I would waste no time in trying to let him know I was feeling him, so in the run up to Valentine's Day, I created the most WONDERFUL card complete with glitter, crepe paper, multi-coloured felt tip penmanship, and even a quick spritz of my mum's Chanel No.5 perfume (soz Mum...) and popped it into a posh envelope to present to him on Valentines' morning. I'd dressed up in my finest, sharpest, gingham school summer dress (pink and white, not blue and white like the other peasants) and had my hair in cute ponytails. I had on my brand-new Clarks Wallabees shoes and they were looking crisp and clean in the cool September air. My face was moisturized with Palmer's Cocoa Butter and I was smelling good. This was it. I was going to land the man of my 10-year-old dreams.

We were going to be boyfriend and girlfriend and go to the same secondary school, then college, then uni. We would go on to create a couples' YouTube channel and make our millions filming ourselves doing various interracial YouTube challenges such as 'My boyfriend uses shea butter for the first time!' and doing 'Meet My Other Half' tags. We were set. I had manifested it and was ready to go!

This was one of the only times in my life where I'd ever taken the courage to approach a man first – the first... and last time, TBH.

SO. Lunch time arrives. I knew exactly where Lewis* was hanging out – by the goalposts opposite the white water fountain (I remember this moment as if it happened yesterday, my friends). I was feeling great, put a bit of tinted Vaseline on my lips and strutted towards him. As I walked towards him, I could see his friends beginning to laugh. Red flag number one.

I then coyly stood in front of him and held up the bright pink envelope; it shook in my hand as I slowly handed it over to him and awaited judgement. Lewis* proceeded to open the envelope and read its contents. He then looked up at me, laughed, called me fat, tore the card into pieces and threw the pieces over me.

That was the day I decided that I would never approach a boy or man first, ever, ever, ever again.

Fast forward 19 years and I still carry this fear of rejection around when it comes to anything to do with dating. Having only ever had one serious relationship, I guess you could say that I am a bit rusty when it comes to this area of my life. I've tried the whole dating scene but nothing tends to ever stick, which leads me to conclude that a large part of the reason why men don't take me seriously, is due to how I look. It couldn't possibly be my personality because it's fucking awesome if we're being honest, and in lieu of my non-conventional looks and the fact that I've never really been seen as attractive, I've had my whole life to work on my personality and be the 'funny, bubbly' character.

I've been on exactly 11 dates in my entire life...*Eleven!* Most of the times, the guys I tend to match with on apps either never message back, unmatch me after five minutes, or have a look at my Instagram (after I've already told them that I'm fat) and then unmatch me soon after. FUN TIMES FOR ALL INVOLVED, HEY?

With the exception of one eventually super rubbish one, all the other dates seemed alright at best, I suppose, but never led anywhere – again with men citing my appearance as a reason for not wanting to get on board. There was one date I went on when the guy left halfway through dinner, stating my weight as the reason why.

The absolute boldness of these men, aye?

There was one I went on which was okay, but I found out after the date was over that he had a fetish for fat womxn and feeding them (which I should have noticed during the date as he kept trying to feed me at very inappropriate times?? Sir pls. We are at an ice skating rink).

There was another recent occasion where I'd gone on a few dates with this 'amazing' guy where I thought he could have been 'the one' – not 'THEE one', but I felt as if the anxieties of dating and my fear of not being liked could be eased a little, as I mistakenly thought we'd had an awesome connection and he seemed to really like me (and likewise) but I found out he had asked someone else to be his girlfriend (after pretending to suffer from mental health issues, claiming he didn't want to 'date' or have a girlfriend in order to work on his 'issues' only three days prior to asking this new girl out. Men; don't do this, because you trivialize mental illness. Just be honest) and had simply used me as a way to tick off 'fat womxn' on his 'types of womxn I want to fuck' checklist. So much for calling himself a woke feminist, right?

Then there was the date I went on where I ended up finding his Twitter feed, only to see that he'd detailed our date from start to finish, saying how unattractive he found me, but was still going to 'try and fuck' me anyway. Needless to say, we didn't bang.

But I wanna talk about a date I went on that really changed the game for me and opened my eyes to how society sees fat womxn. This is the aforementioned tragic date. Grab a cuppa and let's get into it.

The £300 dare

'I can't wait to meet you, Steph. I've even bought you a gift!'

As I minimized the WhatsApp conversation on my phone, I was filled with dread about what the next evening would bring. It was a couple of weeks before Christmas and I was going on my first date since the end of my last relationship, two years ago. To say I was extremely nervous was a severe understatement.

I'd been talking to Robert* (as he shall be called for the remainder of this story) for a couple of weeks after matching each other on a dating app, eventually moving onto WhatsApp, and all seemed to be going well. Since the demise of my last relationship, I'd been a bit wary of the opposite sex and had gone into every new dating app chat with a high degree of scepticism, however, Robert* seemed different...?

He was funny, *seemingly* very intelligent, open-minded, ambitious, and more importantly, accepted and seemed to prefer the fact that I was bigger.

Side note: It seems a bit silly to have to declare something as trivial as one's weight on an app, but due to how a large percentage of plus-size womxn are treated in the dating world, some of us choose to add a note about our weight to our profiles, almost as some kind of 'disclaimer'. It's even worse when your weight intersects with something such as race or gender. I'll touch on this later, but back to the nonsense!

Date night with Robert* finally came around and I was practically bursting into flames with excitement. We'd agreed to meet in Vauxhall, south-west London, for a couple of drinks. I arrived at the venue early and tweeted a cute picture of myself, telling my followers that I was out on a first date, AS YOU DO.

Robert* arrived and the date began. We had a great time during the three or so hours we spent together – we laughed, we exchanged hilarious date-fail stories, we spoke about our families, likes and dislikes...just normal date stuff, you know? He'd even bought me a little ornament for my room as I'd told him I was still doing it up, which was sweet. At the end of the night, we made out and he said he wanted to see me again.

GOOD SO FAR, AMIRITE?

A week later, and hours of speaking on the phone and texting throughout the night, we decided that he'd come over to my flat and we'd watch a few shows while I cooked (I know, I know, rookie mistake; like I said, I am still a dating newbie ok?). Obviously, one thing led to another and we ended up making whoopie.

That was the last time I heard from him.

Cut to a couple of months later when I received an email from a friend of his. Apparently, Robert* had shown my blog to his friends for 'approval', a little before our first date. This friend tells me that in the interests of full transparency (and his own guilt), he thought he should let me know that the reason I had not heard from Robert* since our second date was because he had been dared to 'pull a fat chick' and – upon completing the dare – had won a sum of money his friends had pooled; a lovely 300 quid.

In that moment, I felt sick. A wave of embarrassment and humiliation washed over me, and I went into my bathroom and cried. I had been terrified of meeting and talking to men for fear of them judging my appearance, as this had happened countless times before. As much as I know that I am an awesome person with a lot to offer, I'm also blindingly aware that the way I look is not what mainstream society considers to be 'beautiful', and that's something I always have to think about and carry with me. In the moments while reading the email, I could literally feel my confidence and self-esteem draining away. The self-esteem that I had fought so hard to regain after my last breakup, gone, just like that. Suddenly, I didn't feel human. I felt like somone's gross play-thing, to pick up and leave whenever they wanted, without any regards to my feelings or thoughts. I felt absolutely worthless, and undeserving of love or desire.

What should have been a lovely couple of dates – a bid to improve my confidence and self-esteem while tackling the shark-infested waters of dating – had turned into a teaching moment for me, and definitely made me feel a lot more wary about dating in general and more importantly, trusting men.

Sadly, my story isn't an isolated incident. We've all heard of sick pranks such as the 'pull a pig' game, which involves a group of men daring each other to hook up with the least attractive womxn (in their eyes) in order to gain clout. There are tales as long as my arm from fellow plus-size womxn who have been duped or tricked in this way and after I shared what happened on Twitter, I received a ton of emails from womxn who had been through exactly the same thing. Frankly, a discussion needs to be had about it.

Dating as a plus-size womxn you see, is an exercise rooted more in frustration, anger, and patience than in romance. When you are not being ignored by prospective interests, you are either subjected to humiliation and abuse or you are fetishized for your weight. Either way, the abject failure to consider the feelings of the plus-size womxn in these situations is just another example of the ways in which we are not afforded the luxury of being treated as human beings.

'As plus-size womxn, we are not afforded the same humanity, care, love, and respect as our thinner counterparts.'

The pool seems to be even smaller when you inject race into the equation too, which I'll touch on later.

It highlights the lack of respect that some men have for womxn, particularly if they do not comply with social norms.

As plus-size womxn, we are not afforded the same humanity, care, love, and respect as our thinner counterparts. This can force a monumental drop in confidence and either put us off dating for life or lead us to partake in more casual dating in an effort to prove our worth through sex.

Luckily (or maybe unluckily?), I had already deleted Robert's* number from my phone, after not hearing from him for a couple of weeks, so I had/have no way to contact and chastise him for what he did. I decided to ignore the friend's email and used Twitter to tell my story, in the hope of opening up the conversation about the way plus-size womxn are treated. My aim was to raise awareness, and while I received some amazing, positive feedback, it also came with its share of trolling and horrible comments – almost all from men, who were either laughing at the situation or suggesting I change my appearance in order to be treated better next time.

I like to think that I'm confident enough and maybe numb enough to the whole experience and haven't let it define me as a womxn, but for those of us who are still on our journeys to finding self-love and increasing our confidence, going through an experience where you are basically seen as an experiment can be battering.

Ultimately, what I've concluded is that men seem to undertake these 'pranks' as a way of gaining respect from their male friends at the expense of womxn's feelings. Men need to stop being impressed by this toxic behaviour. It's time to call it out, to hold each other accountable. Would they be as admiring if someone pulled a prank like this on a plus-size relative – on a sister, perhaps, or a cousin? Most of all, it's time to start taking the emotions, perspectives, and feelings of fat womxn seriously. Regardless of body shape, we all deserve to be treated with respect and basic common decency.

Dating as a fat in general – WHEW!

Apologies for quoting the 'Daily Fail' on this occasion, but did you know that the biggest fear men have when it comes to online dating is their date being fat[7]? A sociopath? No problem! Collector of animal bones? Bring it on. A bitch of a bitch? We like a challenge! But let the womxn's clothing size step over a size 18 and suddenly it becomes the biggest problem in Houston.

When I am on these dating sites and apps, I'm always hyperaware that a large majority of men will dismiss me based on my size. On a lot of the dating sites, you have the opportunity to filter out body types; our bodies are grouped into 'good' bodies and 'bad' bodies and if you fall into the so-called 'bad body' type, you're thrown into the incinerator – Veruca Salt style. It's almost as if these apps refuse to take into account the vast and various complex personalities we all have, and match us based on those attributes.

Weight can be such an equalizer when it comes to criticism; it seems like society will not value you on any level if you are fat, and it's not just the thought of being physically unattractive either. You're also seen as stupid, lazy, and perhaps even unable to perform sexually. The judgement that we have towards size is so unfair on BOTH ends of the scale, but fatness is a state of being that we have been conditioned to believe is safe to mock, insult, and openly be disgusted by.

Even if by some super random miracle, a man finds me attractive, I do sometimes worry he will have to face all these questions by his friends as to why – does he *feel* like he has to settle? Does he have a fat girl fetish? Does he just want a girl who is probably so grateful to have a boyfriend she'll be okay with him cheating and treating her with the utmost disrespect? And most times, it often feels as if there's a double standard for slim womxn and bigger men. While I have no doubt that the dating pool for plus-size men may also be a tricky field to navigate,

---

7   https://www.dailymail.co.uk/femail/article-2769315/From-escaping-bathroom-asking-pregnant-The-shocking-reactions-men-abandoned-Tinder-date-overweight.html

men on a whole are 'allowed' to be fat and can still be considered attractive, while it's still a cardinal sin for womxn. THANKS PATRIARCHY!

The shitty, rubbish, sometimes-insecure part of me used to say that I didn't deserve love, sex, or romance because I'm fat, and so anyone who takes the Herculean leap of faith to date me should be vetted very closely first to check that they're sane. I would feel like they needed to fill out a questionnaire before meeting me to make sure they've read the Terms and Conditions, with all my vital statistics on the page in plain sight. I would also (and sometimes still do) always send a link to my Instagram page which features a plethora of full body shots so they knew what they are getting into. It's normally during this stage of talking that I would notice the men begin to ghost, block, or ignore me. I feel like this behaviour of almost trying to justify my weight was the result of years and years of never seeing my body represented anywhere in a positive way. Womxn who look like me in TV shows and movies are always the bumbling, funny, fat friend, as described in the previous media chapter. We have to lose weight in order to find love. We are the comic relief, the food obsessed, the desexualized, maternal character.

Don't get me wrong, I still fear meeting someone for a first date unlike much else; I worry that the man will feel disappointed at best, misled at worst (EVEN THOUGH I HAVE FULL LENGTH PHOTOS ON MY PROFILE. Aren't our brains annoying??). And if they're disappointed, I know there's only one thing they need to say to justify it to others: 'Well, she was a bit of a fatty.'

I would really like to think we've moved past reducing plus-size bodies into their own dating hole; safely cornered away in our own little category as to not be grouped with the coupling of straight-size people. But unfortunately, we seem to be reminded on a daily basis through messages and Direct Messages on social media, that to find me attractive is something that is fetish-based – something I should *apparently* be grateful for because plus-size bodies are still not considered sexy or good enough to date without creating a red flag. (And if you do find me sexy, you should *most definitely* receive a bloody gold star for your 'alleged' wokeness.)

There's this misconception within online dating that fat womxn can't have standards, value, or confidence. We can't just be looking for a date, a hook-up, a brief episode of romance. We don't deserve a chance, we aren't good enough, and we should be happy for any attention that we get.

But I'm also constantly thinking about why I can't just live my best dating life without having my size be proverbially attached to my attractiveness or worth.

I often think about what it's like to date as a straight-sized person and the ability to just put one's interests and wants into a profile. Oh, how it must feel to be matched with someone and not have your weight being the focus of the conversation? What a time to be alive, eh? Being plus-size on the Internet in any capacity is basically a free-forum for people to have opinions and bash you about your weight. The comments I receive online and on dating apps that I find the most offensive are the ones that start with, 'I love BBW girls' or 'I have a thing for big girls'. And to that I always respond, 'Do you write this to thin womxn? Or is it just because I'm fat you want me to feel grateful for this kind of message?'

It's a bit of a sticky one still. Sure there are plus-size friendly apps and things, but a lot of them tend to fall on the fetish-side than anything else, and while I'm sure a lot of people tend to find what they are looking for on there, I just feel uncomfortable being shoved into the 'special interests' corner of the dating world. I want to be able to go on a 'normal' dating site and feel appreciated and – yes – somewhat normal while browsing or talking to men. I want to be able to have the opportunity to change a person's mind or question their biases on bigger bodies. I want potential partners to not see me as a fat womxn, but just as a womxn. Is that too much to ask?

As you're navigating sex and dating as a fat person, please do me a favour and don't forget that you're not someone's free trial or test. You're not an asterisk. And you're certainly not making someone into a hero or star pupil for being into you. You're a person with so much to give to the world regardless of your size. My only dating regret is that it took me an exorbitant amount of time to realize this.

The hypersexualization of fat and black womxn

Hands up if you've ever been referred to as a 'BBW', a 'fat, black goddess' or a dominatrix? Hands up if you're tired of being fetishized by men because of your body shape?

Let's call a spade a spade: darker-skinned black, fat womxn are bottom of the barrel. We virtually have no privileges when it comes to aesthetics. Yes, black womxn have it bad, and fat womxn of all races have it bad, but it's something about being fat, black, AND dark-skinned that takes the biscuit when it comes to social conditioning, especially dating!

Let's take it back:

It's been like this since the Jim Crow era, when fat, black womxn were resigned to playing the 'Mammy' roles and caretakers of the more attractive womxn. Hell, we can even date it back to slavery and the pre-1700s. Black people as a whole were considered animals; primal, ape-like.

Our difference in body shape rendered us inferior to white people. We were hypersexualized and kept in cages, to be gawped at and prodded by white visitors. When Europeans first travelled to Africa in the 17th century, they were shocked that African dress exposed so much skin, even though it was due to the hot climate there. As a result, African womxn were seen as lewd and sexually insatiable.

Let's take Sarah Baartman (described in Chapter One), for example. The way in which she was exhibited like an animal is similar to the type of fetishization of black bodies that continues to the present day.

I've been on dating apps and sites for about two years now and besides the £300 dare date, I haven't really been on any other dates. Why? Well for one, people hardly 'like' or 'match' with me, and when they do, they always seem to be (and I mean ALWAYS) white men who have a fetish for dominating, fat, black womxn. Do you know how tiresome, dehumanizing and disgusting this is?

They wrote you an intro

I like big black women

Hehe I am a romantic too and always wanted a big soft beautiful black lady in my life 🖤

4 minutes ago

To put it basically, fetishization is taking a fully-fledged, well-rounded human and limiting them to one aspect of their being that they don't even have control over. I am being fetishized for being black and plus-size. I'm not being noticed for being a multi-faceted, intelligent, funny, and kind womxn. I am stereotyped as an extra curvy, sexually aggressive, black womxn, and am supposed to be forever grateful that white men even find me remotely beautiful. This stereotype does not exist in real life.

Actual real messages I've received over the past six months

Hey how are you?
Ahah you look beautiful, I have a thing for black girl, and TBH I love your massive boobs :P

And I like a girl with a really large bum aha.

Hey bbe. wanna meet up? I love black bodies.

My fat black queen.
Sit on my face pls.

I want u to sit on my face until I cum on your saggy tits.

You look so dominant.
I want to fuck your rolls.

Mm I have such a thing for
chocolate. U like white guys hun?

Are you a dom?

I've heard black girls are wild in
bed. Wanna prove me right? :-)

You look like a dominant black
queen. I love fat women.

I'm a sub looking for
a black dom.

I'm looking for a fat dominant black.

'All I know is, my black body is a temple – it is beautiful, independent, and mine. It cannot and will not be fetishized.'

The constant fetishization of black, fat womxn is degrading and humiliating at best. In this instance, I'm specifically referring to darker-skinned black womxn, as there can also be complex colourism issues attached to dating, which also makes it incredibly difficult to date.

We aren't seen as human beings. We are othered. Our bodies are considered disgusting to a point where we aren't even considered human anymore. The BBW categories on pornography sites are synonymous to other fetishes such as watersports and other kinky prospects.

Dating apps? Rubbish. Meeting in real life? You're either invisible, or you're the wing womxn.

It's gotten to the point where I've had to resort to downloading incredibly suspect and creepy fat fetish apps in order to be among people who find my body type somewhat attractive, and it does make me feel a bit sick that I've had to resort to this. I'd never meet anyone from these kinds of apps personally, as fat fetishes and feederism isn't my thing, but I always have the thought of 'maybe there will be one person on here I find attractive who *isn't* into all of this fetishy stuff??!!' Alas no. It's still full of incredibly racist, crass messages about my physique.

Obviously, the statement above about people not liking darker-skinned, black, fat womxn is a generalizing statement as I have heard of some plus-sized, darker-skinned, black womxn in genuine loving relationships, albeit very, very rarely. What's a fat to do when, on one hand, you are fetishized by white men, yet on the other, seemingly disliked by black men?

There has been an age-old conversation online between activists and members within body positivity about black womxn not needing body positivity as much as white womxn because our bodies are seen as more attractive.

This, my friends, is a lie.

While it may ring true when you go back to some Afro-Caribbean countries, I live in the United Kingdom of Great Britain and Northern Ireland, and the standards of beauty surrounding what a particular demographic finds attractive is vastly different here. I have never dated, or gone out with, or been chatted up by a black man. At first, I thought it was something to do with me, however, after talking about it online, I realized that it's a specific type of colourism and misogynoir that a lot of other plus-sized, darker-skinned womxn experience too. To some of them, we are too big, and not seen as generally attractive. To some of them, we do not possess the 'right' kind of fat deemed to be attractive. If our fat isn't deposited in our tits, on our hips, in our asses, or on our thighs, we are rendered invisible.

A controversial statement to make? Absolutely, and once again let the records show that I am speaking from *my* personal experiences only! For a while, I wondered whether I was perhaps making excuses or being too reactive to things. However, on the rare occasions where I have expressed this opinion online (because there's nothing I love more than lamenting about my abysmal love life on social media!!!!!!!), I've typically received an overwhelming response from fellow fat womxn who have felt exactly the same way. Strange, huh?

When it comes to being plus-size, I find that black men do prefer fat, white womxn instead of fat, black womxn. Whether it's because black men want to align themselves with whiteness in a bid to improve their lives or social standing within society, or whether they think that black, plus-size womxn are bottom of the barrel, who knows? But this is something I have definitely noticed over the past 10 years or so.

One thing I have had to make peace with over the last couple of years is that while I love myself, and am confident in my abilities and the fact that I know I'm a great person, I know that society (as a whole) doesn't view me and my body as attractive. I know that myself and others will always find it difficult to date regardless of how amazing we may be as individuals and that's something that, unfortunate as it sounds, I just have to make peace with. It's not me being pessimistic, it's just the reality of the situation.

So, what's the end game? Nothing really – I just thought it important to highlight that it's hard out here for a G, and for Gs that look like me, and that in a perfect world, everyone would be judged on the content of their amazing characters as opposed to how they look, but alas.

Also, I think it's important for those of us who are fat and find it difficult to date, to have a place where we can talk about these issues without fear of being spoken down to or spoken to in a condescending way by those who may be a lot smaller, or a lot more conventionally attractive by society's standards. It's gotten to a point now where I can't even be bothered to share my thoughts on the matter without someone telling me that I need to be 'putting myself out there more' or saying that 'there are loads of men who love plus-size womxn out there'. Yeah; the majority of those men are over the age of 50, OR English isn't their first language (which isn't an issue in itself generally, but it does make conversing difficult initially), OR they aren't into plus-size, black womxn, OR they just see us as a fetish and nothing more. Such a great bunch to choose from, huh?

All I know is, my black body is a temple – it is beautiful, independent, and mine. It cannot and will not be fetishized. My black body was something I had to reclaim and learn to love for myself. I love everything about it. I love the way my skin glows in the sunlight, I love my curly hair, soft thighs, and rolls.

My black body is beautiful, wonderful, and mine (and if you wanna slide into a G's direct messages on social media to declare your undying love for me, please do).

Don't just take it from me though. The words that reside within these pages are mostly ripped from my own experiences and thoughts, but I'm only one person. On the following pages are a couple of experiences from fellow darker-skinned, plus-size womxn.

Plus-size womxn on their experiences of dating

'My dating history has been a process of starts and stops. I entered into the dating game very much behind in regards to everyone else I knew. I went on my first date at the age of 21. And now at 28 I sway between bouts of hopeful optimism and resigned discouragement. Right now I'm wallowing in pessimisms as my attempts at dating have once again come to a halt.

The men who typically approach me in real life are the homeless, cornerstore, who knows the last time he took a shower, types. Online, it's usually the ones looking for a hook-up. Either they think I'm an easier conquest or they believe that fetishizing me is a personal turn on. Then there are the men who claim they want to get to know you, but will ghost you for whatever reason. Here is where my self-esteem really takes a battering.

We all know that there is a higher preference for light skinned/latino/white womxn amongst men of colour. Which is fine, whatever. But it does suck for Black womxn because we still remain the least desired race as a whole and as plus-sized womxn that desirability is lowered even more.

I do feel that bigger black womxn are restricted. Specifically black womxn who don't have the "acceptable" plus-sized body type. If you don't have the "flat stomach and fat ass" (thanks Drake) and you don't fall on the smaller spectrum of plus-sized, dating is definitely going to be different for you. Society has a weird way of making bigger womxn feel like we take up too much space and yet are still invisible at the same time. And as black womxn I think this is exasperated even more.'

– Anon, New York

'I feel like I am only ever good for sexual hangouts and not actual dates.

It makes me feel bad about how I look and that I should be grateful someone deems my non-conventional body worthy of being fucked.

In my feminist mind I know that I am worth so much more and deserving of respect and being treated decently but on the inside I still pick at every body flaw and obsess about what I would do if I woke up one morning with half my body weight gone.

It also brings me back to a relative saying, no one wants to marry a liability, in relation to my size and how I have somewhat resigned myself to never expect having a committed relationship.

When I dabbled on apps like Tinder and Bumble, it was mainly white guys between 25–55 asking if I liked white chocolate or saying they would happily have me smother them or saying they'd been to Kenya or South Africa on holiday and saying I reminded them of someone they dated or hooked up with.

So I routinely download them, feel hopeful for three days, delete them and repeat the cycle.

Tried a fetish/swinging site once and all the black dudes were asking if I wanted to do meet ups with white cuckold couples so I decided to stick to erotic fiction.

I find the scene a struggle because it feels like the rule book has only one chapter dedicated to us and it was written by a size 12 Insta influencer without a FUPA and then promptly edited down to make room for other more supposedly deserving bodies.

I feel hindered because for me, likely because I don't have a strong real life social circle, I depend on non conventional means of meeting people like Tinder/ Bumble etc., where people tend to – because they're not interacting face to face – allow their humanity filter to be on a much lower setting.

I hate having to add I am plus-size as a warning label in my profiles and that no race fetishists are welcome. Also the fact that I rarely come across singles/mixer nights geared toward us outside London does feel a bit isolating.

I hate how I feel I am taking up too much space if I slip into a booth at a restaurant and feeling like I am being watched and judged when I order carbs instead of a salad.

I feel like men and society need to stop touting that real black/African womxn are bigger but only with a small waist, big boobs and flat stomach and loose curly hair.

There's a spec out there and when you don't meet it any form of tenderness is eked out in tiny infrequent doses.'
– Ada, London

'I'm divorced with a daughter and have had one failed long-distance situationship since being divorced.
I accepted behaviours and excuses that I know I shouldn't accept but convinced myself that I was just being bitter. I believe at the time I wasn't fully healed (post-divorce dating – I married my college sweetheart) and rushed into something just to claim him I think. It wasn't the smartest decision but since then have been in therapy and am now actively dating.

Online, BBW fetish lovers who are more than likely married or have a secret family. They have a TON of preconceived notions about womxn (some of them love to refer to womxn as "females") It's a scary world out there!

Being black and big has huge drawbacks because the men you want, go for the big white womxn. My ex-husband left me for one so I am absolutely certain that I'd bag a guy tomorrow. Not sure if he'd be a quality dude, but he'd be bae in no time. Something about big white womxn gets a lot of black men excited for some odd reason. Also, Hispanic womxn (I live in Fort Lauderdale, Florida) they're a hot ticket as well. Like they get the best of both worlds in their mind. Being black and a womxn is tough in dating... being black, BIG and a womxn? Huge handicap.

With plus-size dating, you're not too sure if the person you're attracted to is attracted to you. I oftentimes run into men who say they're into big girls or "womxn" and then start talking to you and want to "change your lifestyle" or "help you feel better about yourself" as if you were wallowing in plus-size self-pity all your life. It's annoying. I do not feel like I'm unattractive or that I can't get a dude to like me because I also know that plus-size loving is a bit trendy now and I'm in my thirties. The men I run into or pursue are in my age range or older and tend to be attracted to me from the beginning plus my

*personality is pretty cool which is an added bonus for
their dating struggles.*

    *Plus-size dating is hard to navigate but always make
sure to love all of you before you try and love anyone else.
Never get in a relationship with anyone feeling bad in your
body. Somebody will always like it and love it and want
more of it. Being plus-size doesn't mean you shouldn't be
seen and loved on publicly. It means you deserve to get
the finest of man in your corner cheering you on cuz you
a slice of heaven and he's blessed to have you in it.
Always know that.'*

– Nefertiti, Fort Lauderdale

*'I wouldn't describe myself as a successful dater because I
lack the confidence to actually go on a date. I feel as though
I am catfishing because online me knows how to take
the perfect selfies showing my best angles which means
attempting to hide my rolls of fat or holding my phone just
that bit higher to not show my almost double chin.*

    *It's frustrating that I let my insecurities of being fat
get in the way of meeting men, but society has made me
feel that men only like womxn if they have the fat in the
right places i.e. curvy hourglass and my fat is not that.*

    I tend to attract older black men in their forties.

    *Online – all sorts. But usually guys who probably
wouldn't look twice at me in the street. Sometimes I get
bored and so upload a casual selfie with a bit of boob
showing and men are so predictable that invariably, I
will get an inbox from some thirsty person. I'll entertain
it (if they look somewhat appealing and aren't incredibly
odd from glancing at their profile) for a time.*

    *I honestly do feel like it would be easier to date
if I were plus-size and white.'*

– Annalisa, Sheffield

So, You're Fat and You Wanna Date

Dating online when you're plus-size. If you're someone who is good at getting dates IRL, well done! You'll probably be able to skip this bit to be honest, but for those of us who are trawling the apps for the loves of our lives, here are a few tips when logging on to make the process as anxiety-free as possible:

Always include a FULL LENGTH photo of yourself. One of the OG rules of online dating: please do not give these men any excuse to shame you. Often times, plus-size womxn are accused of catfishing more than anyone else, even if we are who we say we are – because men feel like they've been 'betrayed' or finessed when only exposed to facial photos or photos that cut off just above the bust.

Optional: Mention your body type in your profile. This is admittedly, a bit of a controversial one. In an ideal world, no one should ever have to mention their weight, or their height for that matter as some kind of 'disclaimer'. It's the least important thing about us when looking for a potential mate but in the times that we live in now, I feel that by adding something along the lines of 'fatter IRL' or something funny like that, it actually weeds out all the fuckboys and people who would otherwise waste your time, and attract you to people who either prefer larger womxn, or are attracted to people regardless of weight (i.e., the non-fuckboys).

If they mention your weight more than your personality, they may not be the one. Now this totally depends on your personal preferences. If you are someone that is into the BBW/feederism fetish lifestyle, then totally miss this one out. If the potential partner keeps banging on about your body in either a harmful, gross, or hypersexual way, however, you may have found yourself someone with a bit of a fetish, who is intent on reducing your lovely self down to a sexual vessel. It may be time to abandon ship.

If they mention your skin colour (regardless of how 'cute' the compliment may be), they also may not be the one. Look we've all heard those lines. 'My chocolate Queen', 'Aww your skin colour turns me on', 'my caramel Goddess', 'MY BLACK RUBENESQUE APHRODITE!'...yeah. These are all pretty clear signs that someone is trying to fetishize your skin colour, and I would also stay clear if I were you. Equally though, if you are into that kind of thing and have the relevant self-care tools to help process this kind of fetishism (both racially and in body weight) then by all means go for it!

Be confident and don't bring up your weight if you can help it. Yep, yep, I know I literally just said that mentioning weight in your profile could be a good thing, but this tip is for when you are getting to know the person and hanging out a lot more. The more you keep saying things like *'are you sure you like me at this weight?'*, *'I can't believe you said yes to coming on a date with me, despite how I look'*, and *'are you sure you like me?'* the more it'll come off as incredibly insecure, which is a bit of a turn off.

Dress comfortably. Don't feel as if you have to go all out for the person. You're not meeting Jesus – you're meeting a randomer you've just met online. Now, I'm not going to tell you exactly what to wear as style is subjective and frankly, you can wear whatever feels good on you, but as long as it's comfortable. Personally, I love anything with a square neckline – it's quite a formal look, but it gives you a generous flash of cleavage that I really like. Crop tops and A-line skirts with Chelsea boots are another fave of mine, as well as A-line skirts combined with blouses or tops with padded shoulders, to balance out my smaller bottom half!

First Date? Opt for somewhere very public and well lit. Now, these are no-brainers and can be applied to anyone regardless of weight, but try and find a venue that has a considerable amount of people in order to lessen that first-date anxiety. I always show up at least 10 minutes before date time too, as I feel more comfortable not making that first entrance and seeing the light fade in their eyes as I draw nearer...

EAT. Look, we've all been there. Years ago, I absolutely hated eating in front of people for fear of what they would think, but you know what, go for it. You're a human being who needs nourishment too, and you shouldn't allow yourself to feel ashamed for doing something literally every other person on this earth does, and if your date has a problem with you eating, they can get in the bin too.

Don't pressure yourself to dress up. When you're fat, it's often commonplace when dating that we wear pieces of clothing that enhance the areas of our bodies that are often hypersexualized, e.g. our boobs, bums, and thighs, while minimising the 'non-sexy' parts of ourselves such as our tummies and side fat, etc. To that I say – fuck THAT. We don't have time. Look, I get that having the hourglass shape is marketable. Growing up, we've been told that there is no other acceptable 'curvy' shape than the hourglass, but it's okay to not feel the pressure to present yourself in that way if you don't have to. When I first took my foray into the dating world, I'd always wear something that showcased my boobs. Why? Because I felt that I had to perform femininity, seeing as that's what men liked' but that's not the case my friends. Dress in whatever you feel comfortable in!

Most importantly, learn how to love yourself and your body. Cliché , I know! Telling someone that they need to learn how to love themselves before they can invite that positive romantic energy into their lives is a tale as old as time (and is something I'm personally still trying to do!) but it works, trust me. When you start falling in love with your body, you become more fearless. You take more chances with your style choices. You hold your stature differently when in public. You become more confident and invite positive energy into your space, which can then invite the right person into your life?!

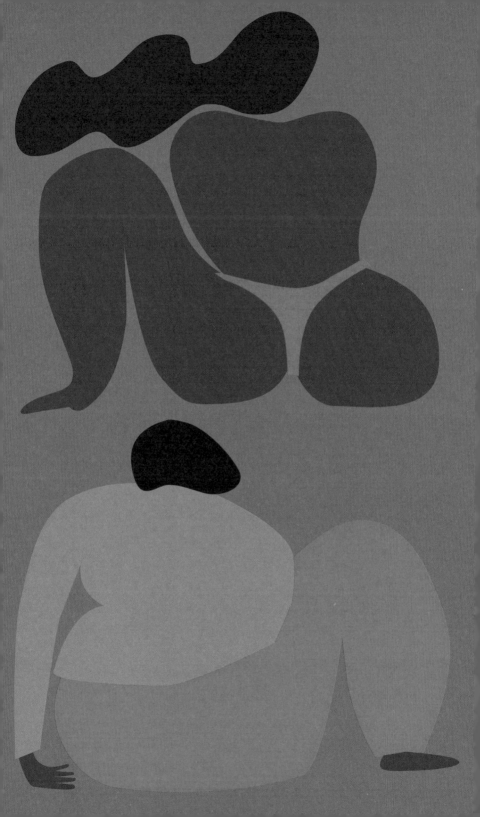

Chapter FOUR

Desexualization Or Hypersexualization –

What Is The TRUTH?

The tragic tale of the skater hoodie and disco flares from Peacocks

Growing up, I'd probably say that I was a bit of a tomboy. I loved video games. I loved comic books. I hated dressing up in 'girly' clothes for the most part, and a lot of my time was spent (especially when I used to live in Ghana) climbing up trees and playing with the boys.

Equally, I also started collecting copies of *Vogue* and creating collages on my wall which would feature my very own 'couture line' from the age of about 13. Alongside taking part in what society would consider 'masculine' horseplay as a child, I would also always come home from secondary school every day, pop the cable on and tune into my favourite channel: Fashion TV.

I was absolutely crazy about fashion. The creativity, the drama, the fabulous gowns, the beautiful models, and the outlandish camaraderie of it all. I was mad for it!

You'd never know by looking at the way I dressed, however. The entirety of my secondary school life consisted of absolute fashion fails; it was like my wardrobe was on crud, mate. I would wear a bandana to school every day to cover up my damaged hair which had been the result of having a home-styled Jherri-curl. Alongside said bandana – which by the way, came in an assortment of different colours because I was still trying to look cute – was a pair of those ghastly disco/grunge flared, denim jeans with a racing stripe down the sides of both legs. I used to buy these jeans in bulk from Peacocks – one of the very few brick-and-mortar stores on this island called the UK, that somewhat catered to plus-size bodies at the time.

Alongside these jeans would be hoodies in multiple colours. My secondary school didn't really adhere to a strong uniform policy, so the kids would usually rock up wearing school uniform-adjacent clothing.

This would be my go-to uniform. Trying to cover up as much of myself as possible in order to 'look' smaller. It was almost my way of unintentionally desexualizing myself because I knew that someone of my size couldn't possibly be found attractive by the boys, so why try and accentuate my body even more when I was already considered invisible?

I think that it was also a very strong reason as to why I identified as a tomboy and hung out with boys too; why I took up interest in subjects typically projected towards boys than girls, such as sci-fi and graphic novels. Growing up, not only was it virtually impossible to find plus-size, black womxn to admire and look up to, but when they did come around, they would always be positioned as somewhat aggressive or masculine-presenting in some way. For the longest time, I just thought that's how we were meant to present ourselves.

I didn't acknowledge the presence of dresses or how they would ever relate to me until I started my blog, to be honest. Even back then while at uni, I would wear my favourite Primark leggings with cold-shoulder, butterfly blouses and long smock tops that looked like something straight out of an OAP clothing catalogue. I'd normally finish the look with a pair of Chelsea boots, or some trainers. Getting me to wear a dress back then would have been like getting Azaelia Banks to apologize for shading other rappers and singers online. Impossible...absolutely impossible. Not only was it difficult to find dresses that would actually fit me well but would also be current and stylish enough for people to not assume that I was some kind of foreign exchange student from an unidentifiably random place.

Mama's first dress!

Once ASOS opened their Curve range, however, that was IT. ASOS Curve opened up a whole new world for me in terms of clothing and how I felt towards my body, as coincidentally it was during the same time that I had discovered the body positivity community online, had fallen in love with plus-size bloggers, and was going through my journey of self-love and learning how to un-learn toxic, fatphobic traits. My blog was going from strength to strength, and so I decided to introduce plus-size fashion as a new category on there, by way of purchasing my first ever 'proper' dress. It was a rust coloured polka dot dress that I had seen on my favourite plus-size fashion bloggers, Nicolette Mason and Gabi Gregg. The dress just looked so elegant and flawless on them, so I thought, 'Why not try it on me?'.

I tried the dress on and to my surprise, I didn't immediately hate it. The dress outlined my shape without drawing attention to the fact that I wasn't hourglass shaped. It was short and so allowed my long naked legs to flourish. It was...weird, seeing me look so...*feminine.* Up until that point, I had been so accustomed to the idea that black, fat womxn had to be strong, masculine, aggressive, and show no signs of being sexual, so to see myself in this new light was incredibly illuminating for me.

I remember taking almost 800 photos of me from every angle in that dress. I wanted to see what my boobs looked like, my thighs, my hips, and my bum. It almost felt like I was watching myself become a womxn physically for the first time all over again. My boobs were THAT big? How could I have missed how long and lean my legs were? Did I actually look...attractive in this garment? I had so many questions running through my head. The idea of me presenting as feminine was something I struggled with, and it took me a long time to un-learn the ideology that had brainwashed me for years about it. I bought a couple more dresses in different styles, in order to see how my body looked. I bought a couple of A-Line dresses, some tulip dresses (which I found did not work for my shape at all), big, bouncy, floral dresses that exaggerated my hips, and even bodycon dresses which actually ended up making me feel incredibly uncomfortable, as it allowed

'YOU!!! DO!! NOT!!! OWE!!! ANYONE!!! FEMININITY!!'

me to finally see my body shape for what it was, not the stereotypical 'hourglass' curvy shape that black womxn were 'supposed' to have (which we will cover in an upcoming chapter).

Alongside following my favourite femme plus-size bloggers and buying dresses, I started wearing makeup a lot more too. I started experimenting with bright lipsticks and winged eyeliner – I had finally unlocked this level of my life and I wanted to jump balls-deep into it and discover what it meant to be, and feel, feminine. All my life I had been subconsciously pushed into this desexualized corner, gently prodded by images that I'd see on the television, from what I'd seen in society, and from being around boys and seeing the stark contrast in how they spoke about the slim, ultra-feminine girls and how they would speak to me. It was my time, my time right now, to discover what it meant to be, and act, feminine.

So, I gotta wear a corset now??

So, the whole 'me in dresses' thing was going along swimmingly for a while. I was blogging more about my favourite floral prom dresses, talking about how flattering they were on specific parts of my body and what have you, but then I began noticing something about the way in which plus-size womxn – especially black, plus-size womxn – were being presented online. All of a sudden, it was 'hourglass' this and 'hourglass' that. Tits up to here and a butt down to there. The tummies were getting smaller and the hips were getting wider.

I'd go onto social media sites such as Tumblr, to see beautiful black, plus-size womxn flaunting their curves, but it seemed to be a specific type of curve that was being celebrated now – the exaggerated hourglass figure. I started to compare myself to these womxn, thinking that I too needed to have that shape in order to qualify as a 'good fat'. After all, black womxn were 'supposed' to have the big tits and big butts, right? It's a part of #our #culture to be shaped in such an exaggerated way.

So, I ended up buying a corset from some shoddy website online. I am not well versed in corset lore and didn't buy the right one for my size, as I assumed you treated corsets the same way you'd treat a girdle and just size down by a couple of sizes.

Big mistake, lads.

The corset arrived looking like some kind of medieval instrument of torture, and it took about 18 attempts, near asphyxiation, and a bruised torso before I could finally fasten the damned thing onto my torso. Pain aside, I forced myself to wear the corset every day – to train my waist, if you will – because in my head I thought that in order to be seen as an attractive and 'acceptable' fat, one had to adhere to the correct and ultra-specific body dimensions that proved popular within society.

The corset survived a grand total of two weeks before I chucked it in the bin, my friends.

It consistently felt like I had an anaconda around my middle at all times, and although I would have somewhat of an 'hourglass-ish' adjacent shape when I wore it, I never quite got there – my waist simply wouldn't allow it!

I always struggled with the fact that there seemed to be only two ways to 'present' as a fat womxn, and more specifically, a fat, black womxn: we were either portrayed as hypermasculine, or overly maternal and desexualized, hypersexualized and hyperexaggerated. There seemed to be no middle ground where I could just exist as a 'normal' fat womxn who could present herself in whatever way she deemed fit. I wanted to be normal, but as a lot of us who reside in these bodies know, there is hardly such a thing as 'normal' when you exist in a body that society has taught you to hate from birth.

I'm just doing me, babe

Nowadays, I try not to pay attention to what society deems beautiful or not. It isn't always easy though, and I'm always trying to un-learn toxic thoughts and behaviours anytime I recognize it. For example, I'm a huge fan of mum-jeans, right? For a while though, I quit wearing jeans and trousers as much, for fear of men assuming that I may be too 'masculine' and therefore not wanting to approach me. I know, I know...weird thinking and it's annoying that these tropes exist, but the sad fact is they do. We've always been subtly told by the media that the pin-up is glamorous. Sexy. It's 'womxnly' in its celebration of the curves we are constantly told to play up to. Exaggerated hip there. Tucked in waist. Mahoosive boobs! As a fat womxn, I've lived through most of my life being told that I'm less of a womxn because of my size. Beauty, glamour, and sexiness have all been denied me because I've simply been 'too big' for them.

When you are black, you are ALREADY labelled (consciously or unconsciously) by society as aggressive, powerful, sassy, and masculine. Being fat on top of that does little to change that. From black womxn's earliest days in this patriarchal Western world, we have been branded as wanton and sexually aggressive sirens — Jezebels — a far cry from white womxn who were, for the most part, seen as inherently pure. This assumption of black womxn's freakiness and hypersexuality runs deep, and it leaps in large part from the antebellum era in the United States, when enslaved womxn were routinely subjected to sexual violence and white plantation owners sought to justify it. Centuries later, black female sexuality is still the source of moral panic because change takes ages, and stereotypes — especially entrenched ones — are exceptionally hard to undo. I suspect some of my white peers can relate to what I'm describing. And it's true that womxn of all colours and races face the challenges of sexual expectations. But the pervasive stereotype that black womxn in particular are hypersexual adds a whole other area of stress.

It just feels like we can never meet in the middle when it comes to our femininity. On one hand, we are expected to be desexualized and maternal a-la all the Mammy tropes we are so used to growing up seeing on TV. On the other hand, because we have this stereotype as aggressive and masculine, there is also this expectation that we must perform masculinity and be 'one of the lads'. Failing that, the only other route is being 'hyperfeminine' in order to prove that your fatness is worth being seen as beautiful and valid.

Can we not exist within all categories?

Give me chinos, baggy jeans, boxy shirts, or dungarees any day of the week. I'll wear them while beating you at Mario Kart and still be able to knock your socks off in a gorgeous Playful Promises lingerie set!

Femininity does not equal validity

Say it with me:

'YOU!!! DO!! NOT!!! OWE!!! ANYONE!!! FEMININITY!!'

From hypermasculinity to hyperfemininity: I've said it before, and I'll say it again, the level of femininity that fat girls have to perform in order to not be seen as ugly or weird is absolutely phenomenal.

Femininity is not a bad thing, however, I really do detest the idea that fat womxn are only seen as attractive within society when we are wearing lingerie, or have a face full of makeup on, or when we have a sultry expression on our faces.

Don't get me wrong, the aforementioned are all things that are valid, as fat womxn deserve to feel sensual and to explore our sexuality in all forms, however, the problem occurs when it becomes the standard by which society uses to judge all fat people in order to be seen as socially attractive, or to cement physical validation. It also dangerously treads into the pornographic category, in which plus-size womxn are stripped of their humanity for the most part and are seen as a tool for the pleasure of men under the guise of the 'BBW' and 'SBBW' fetish tags.

We shouldn't have to justify our validity and self-worth by conforming to the ultra-femme ideal. This isn't to say that being ultra-femme in itself is wrong. I completely understand that it is a label and a lifestyle that a lot of womxn identify with and it is completely valid in its own right, however, it's important to also recognize that we can be attractive, sexy, cute, and valid wearing no makeup and oversized clothes, as well as in a hot piece of lingerie.

The subject of sexuality and weight is definitely something that has been fed to us through the eyes of the patriarchy. On one hand, it's easy to see why as fat womxn, we sometimes lean into performing hyperfemininity in order to be 'seen' as attractive by society. Let's think about it:

take a photo of a slim womxn with A or B cup boobs and put her in a spaghetti strap dress or a low V-neck top, and that's acceptable. Now take a plus-size womxn with size DD breasts and some extra hip action, and suddenly, in comes the onslaught of crude and horrible comments. Suddenly Instagram flags the post up for 'indecent content' and people begin to flag the photo as inappropriate.

Why? Because extra skin is seen as more sexual. As your thighs get thicker and your butt gets rounder, the length considered acceptable for shorts, skirts, or dresses goes way down when you're fat. If we exude a kind of hyperfemininity at all times, at least we'll be slightly more palatable. We'll remind people that not only are we worthy of our womxnhood, but of our basic humanity, too.

Another possible reason why fatness is so hyper-sexualized is because of the old beauty standards; during the Renaissance era for example, having a 'Rubenesque' body was all the rage. You would see paintings and sculptures featuring womxn with rolls and large bellies, and it was seen as a thing of beauty. It reminded me of a short story I came across when researching for my book, called *Boule de Suif (Ball of Fat)*, by Guy de Maupassant, who was a famous author. In this book, the protagonist was the hero of the novella; she was a curvy prostitute, whose physical description used three different lexical fields: food metaphors, fat/roundness, and sexual desire. When reading it, I got a feeling of both disgust and appeal, and it feels like sometimes when existing in society as a plus-size womxn, that it is the same disgust and hypersexual appeal that is projected onto me, and even maybe what I project onto myself at times.

Female nudity, I think in general, is transgressive, although our level of tolerance has slowly increased, due to online platforms such as Instagram, Twitter and, of course, #FEMINISM. However, showing 'too much' of your body when you're fat is perceived as a much bigger transgression. One look at the comments section of a Fat Acceptance article in the *Daily Mail* will show you. On a subconscious level, interiorized fatphobia says it should stay hidden. And it's mainly the transgressive part that's so hypersexual.

Femininity and gender

Fat womxn can be feminine. *But it isn't the be all and end all.* We can be other things too. We can be alternative. We can be androgynous. We can be gender non-conforming and non-binary. We can be butch. We can be casual. We can be all these things and STILL have the right to exist and feel socially acceptable within society. For instance, to be fat and gender non-conforming is to explicitly, physically go against what is expected of you by societal prejudices and expectations. These expectations impose restrictions on people, which can have painful, damaging consequences.

The ongoing fight for radical fat acceptance and the fight for the acceptance of butch, trans, and gender non-conforming people are separate movements that largely don't interact in the public sphere. Even within the body positivity and radical fat activism spaces, in order to deem them beautiful, we are still expected to make up for this perceived 'flaw' of fatness, which is an equal strike against non-binary people, trans people, and gender non-conforming womxn in general. I think that such a high level of femininity is demanded of fat womxn typically, and it's been a struggle for those who do not identify as such, trying to understand that not only the 'traditional' feminine is sexy.

Within the plus-size community, it is important to showcase and lift up people who do not fall within the hyperfemme tag, because *all bodies matter*, regardless of whether it's being shown in a pretty peek-a-boo bra or not.

113

You Do Not Have to Conform

Even though we still have an incredibly long way to go in regards to recognising and highlighting true diversity and celebrating individuality, it's nice to be living in a time where fat womxn have a bit more freedom to be who they want to be, and showcase to the world that we matter. Here are a couple of things you can do that may help alleviate the pressures of having to perform femininity:

Follow a wide range of fat acceptance activists online. The current state of the Body Positivity movement at the moment is just...it's shit's creek ok? Full of small/ acceptable fat femme womxn trying as much as possible to contort their body in order to create a roll. You don't need any of that. Personally, I would miss that hashtag altogether, as I feel like it could potentially do more harm than good. For content that hosts an array of different fat body types and genders, the #radicalfatactivism #factacceptance and #radicalfatacceptance hashtags seem to be the best ones I've found.

Watch ethical porn if you can. Look, we're all adults here and we've all come across a Pornhub or two in our time! It's well known that pornography caters to the patriarchy, and puts their needs first. For the most part, womxn are displayed as mere tools for pleasure, and are dressed up and presented in ways for the benefit and pleasure of men. Over the last couple of years, however, we have been seeing a growing number of ethically-made porn material, with videos being made by female directors, porn that focuses primarily on female enjoyment, and ethical companies who make the performers' wellbeing a top priority. There is less focus on dressing up and presenting for the male gaze, and instead, focusing on our needs and what we want. Websites such as Four Chambers, Eroticfilms.com, Joybear, and PinkLabel contain a mixture of free and pay-to-play videos that are feminist, gender-inclusive with strong, multi-dimentional womxn characters, and are predominantly made by womxn directors. I'd definitely give these a try.

Report damaging ads on social media. Far be it for me to want to damage anyone's businesses online, but if you are scrolling along Instagram and see an ad promoting things such as waist trainers, I personally would report the page. In 2019, Instagram finally took a stand and banned these types of ads from being seen by users under the age of 18, so it shows that small changes are being made, but there is so much more that can be done. Stars such as Kim Kardashian have increased the marketability of waist trainers[8] – which can be incredibly harmful if not used under the supervision of a doctor for medical reasons – and which are now promoted on Instagram to create a super dramatically exaggerated hourglass shape. This has led to an influx of bogus companies claiming to give you the 'hourglass body you've always dreamed of'. BALLS TO THAT. All it is doing is force feeding you a completely unrealistic standard of beauty while simultaneously trying to asphyxiate you. I'll say it again: an exaggerated hourglass shape is NOT a realistic standard of beauty. You do NOT have to have this shape in order to be considered beautiful!

Have fun with fashion, because it's not that deep. This piece of advice is as much for me as it is for you because I remember being completely obsessed with how certain outfits would make me look, and whether I would be femme enough to pass.

---

8   https://www.refinery29.com/en-us/are-waist-trainers-dangerous

'Is this dress an A-line dress?'

'Will it nip me in at the waist?'

'Can you see my VBO?'

'Will a flannel shirt give off the impression that I don't really care about my appearance?'

'Should I be wearing oversized T-shirts as a fat womxn?'

'Are these jeans a bit "too" baggy?'

Trust me, I used to have whole checklists of things I would need to tick off before leaving my house. Over the years, however, I've accepted that fashion is there for us to have fun with it. Unless you're a fashion designer, it's really not 'that' deep. Have fun creating different looks, regardless of if it makes you look a specific way or not. At the end of the day, you have to remember that unless you're an actor in a really dope play or TV show, you're dressing for you, and no one else. Show up for yourself and give the best performance you can hunny!

Word search

```
F W S E S Q U M B P C T
M S T Q S E S R E D U A
W O R U O Y T K A T R O
F E O C F D R N U H V B
A T N B T L N R T B Y A
T H G T F S O T Y U M B
Q A P W Y X G Z N T C E
C T A G P O W E R F U L
M H K Z X A R O B E G D
F I O G O R G E O U S G
S C W P D E L A N E I P
E K E T S T R E T C H W
```

* **Beauty**   * **Thick**
* **Fat**   * **Strong**
* **Stretch**   * **Soft**
* **Curvy**   * **Powerful**
* **Babe**   * **Gorgeous**

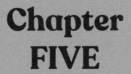

Chapter
FIVE

36-24-36?
In This
Economy?!

In July 2018, I logged onto the Internet to do my evening routine of reading some of my favourite blogs when I came across a blog post written by one of my favourite content creators and fellow Ghanaian, Chanel Ambrose. The post was entitled 'My Unpopular Body Shape'.

The blog post in question revolved around the fact that Chanel never felt as if she ever fit in growing up, because she felt she had 'the wrong body'. Below is an excerpt of the blog post in which she finds a comment on her YouTube page, no doubt from some 'concerned follower':

'I then stumbled across a comment that literally shook me to infinity.

The comment said "Your ass shape is not normal for a black girl. You're still beautiful though, I like the clothes you have shown, you are putting on so much weight, try to lose some weight."'

I remember reading this blog post and being shaken to my absolute core, because it was so interesting to see that I wasn't the only one who had these thoughts about the stereotypical African body shape and how it feels to not conform to that standard, through no fault of your own.

'Ooo, I wish I had a black womxn's figure...', 'White womxn are getting bum implants to try and look like black womxn – the standards of beauty have changed'.

I'm beginning to hear these statements all the time and I've always thought, what does it mean to look like a black womxn? Deep down, we all know the answer, or at least we think we do. Apparently, we are all supposed to have big arses and small waists. We just don't talk about our beauty standards and it's high time that we, as black womxn and plus-size, black womxn, started having a conversation about our bodies, because the mainstream body positivity movement isn't – and has no intention of doing so any time soon.

'Mum, what happened to my bum?!'

I often get asked the question, 'Even though you are body positive and preach a lot about self-love and body confidence, if you had the option to have free surgery, would you have it, and where?' (Why I get asked this? I have no reason why – my Instagram pals are a funny lot!)

My answer to that is, 'On a somewhat bad day, I absolutely would. I'd get a BBL (Brazilian Butt Lift) which involves taking fat from one area of the body and sticking it into the butt, increasing the size. I just want a big arse. A big ole' ignorant, ridiculous butt that I can gyrate to my hearts' content. I want to be able to twerk on my knees along to Megan THEE Stallion and not feel as if I'm overdoing my hips in a bid to keep up with the wobble. I want to be able to fill up a pair of jeans without there being a weird sag right in the middle of my bum. IT'S WHAT I DESERVE, DAMNIT!

Growing up, I'd never really been aware of the *type* of body shape I had, as I was hyperaware of the fact that I had too much body in the first place. I think I was around 14 when I noticed that my plus-size body shape was different to the other black, thick, and curvy body shapes I'd see on TV.

Even though I'm fat, I wouldn't necessarily say that I have the stereotypical shape that black womxn are 'supposed' to have. I do not have an hourglass-shaped figure. I don't have the small waist that slopes into rounded, full hips and a rounded bum. Sure, I have the boobs, but I'd like to think that those assets are pretty broad, TBH. What I wanted was the BUTT. How could I feel a part of the community if I didn't have the one thing that I thought would give me the most attention? How could I feel like a #real #womxn if I didn't have the curves that would validate me?

Around the age of 14, I started comparing my body to the bodies of others at school. I would notice that the boys would go crazy over the 'bumpahs' of the girls and how big they were, meanwhile, I was carrying around this sack of nothing. I remember asking my mum why I hadn't inherited her figure. My mum is pretty petite and while she isn't shaped like Nicki Minaj, her body is still pretty well-rounded and hourglass shaped. I wondered why her genes hadn't been passed on to me. Hell, even my brother has a bum! Of all people! I was mad as hell.

I was always told that my bum may come in if I lost a bit of weight, and so I held onto that. I tried to start dieting in a bid to 'improve' my silhouette and somehow try and claim some kind of booty. I would go to Weight Watchers and count my calories every day, use kettlebells to try and strengthen my core and add muscle to my butt, and would use body shapers around my middle to try and create an hourglass shape, but to no avail. My body wasn't having it.

Eventually I had to accept that I was never going to have the shape that I desired and honestly...it made me pretty fucking upset!

Throughout my teens, I would often travel back home to Ghana to see family during the six-week school vacation. There were a variety of reasons why I sometimes hated going back: the heat, the fact that I would force myself to wear leggings and cardigans in spite of said heat lest anybody look at my fat body, the spiders and mosquitos constantly knocking about, but mostly, I hated the criticism of my body from relatives and friends of relatives. OH, HOW I HATED IT!

I was ALREADY a pretty quiet teenager up until that point and for some reason, it made me even more of a target for questioning and critiquing:

'Steph, why are you so quiet?'

'You're always on your laptop, this is why you're gaining weight.'

'Ayeeeeee *OBOLOBO*!!' – 'obolobo' is a Twi word which means 'fat'.

'You should try and lose weight on your top half

because your bottom half is so much smaller.'

'How are you going to get a husband if you have so much weight? It's not good at all.'

Every single time I would hear this, it made me want to shrink further into the floor. A lot of people tend to assume that fatphobia is virtually non-existent in Africa, and that to be fat over there means that the said fat person is wealthy, healthy, and highly regarded. While there may be some truth to this assumption (especially back in the day), it was something that never rang true for me, nor for other African womxn I've spoken to.

Sure, being bigger may seem like a bit of a comfort and a break from the ultra-unrealistic Westernized standards of beauty – but again – if you're not shaped in a specific way or have fat in the places that are deemed as hypersexual, you'll still be exposed to the same amount of shame. At least that was my experience. I was always told that no man would find me attractive being the weight I was, and why didn't I have the same pear shape as my mum. It would be a constant barrage of opinions that I would internalize and transform into self-hate for years to come.

The unfortunate case of the lopsided butt pads

College and university didn't really help either. The lads would be hitting up raves and parties each week and I would purposely not go because I just hated how I looked in a bodycon dress. I mention bodycon dresses as back in my day, Herve Leger had just re-released his legendary Bandage dress and so, imitation dresses were all the rage.

Nevertheless, my quest for trying to get a big butt continued, I'm sad to say. I remember going online and finding out about these wondrous products called butt pads. Apparently, ALL the celebs used them. They were just like chicken fillets, except they fit into this bit of shapewear similar to a girdle, which you wore over your knickers. No pain. No surgery. Seemed simple enough. I bought a pair and waited with such excitement: I'd already planned out the outfits I was going to wear them in and – teamed with my corset – I was going to create the hourglass-shaped body to end all bodies. I was finally going to fit in with the rest of my peers!

So, the day came! I was waiting by the door for the Amazon delivery guy. Why is it they take so long to arrive when you NEED something urgently BTW? Don't they know that we have things to do?! As soon as he arrived, I tore open the packaging and simply gazed at my new prize in awe. It was perfect! The pads contained two silicone moulds that were HUGE and sat inside the inserts in the back of the 'girdle'. I made sure to get a skin toned colour so it could blend in seamlessly with my skin. Anyhoo, I popped it on to see how it fit and...well...it was something, alright. It was weird, seeing myself with this extra junk in the trunk. I slid a dress on top to see the finished result and without being dramatic, I absolutely fell in love...10/10 would have recommended. It's weird, at the time, although I was generally unhappy with my body shape, it felt like I at least had this silver lining – this acceptable body part that would validate my fatness and make me appear more desirable to men??

I started wearing the butt pads to uni classes most days a week, and again when we would go out to bars around the town. I felt somewhat powerful, and more confident than I had ever been in years (even though I was still crippled under the humongous wave of self-hate). I was wearing tighter clothes (to a point), I was dancing out in public a lot more and, in general, I just felt really, really good.

Here comes the fuckery.

One night myself and a couple of mates took our arses down to the legendary hotspot that was Oceana in Kingston (the institution, the myth, the legend that is) for some good times, as we'd heard that Bobby Valentino was rumoured to be playing there that evening.

I put on my trusty butt pads and threw on this sparkly scuba dress thing I bought from Marks & Spencer, I believe. It was cute, form-fitting, but not too close to the skin. And it was pretty short, so I loved it.

So, we go off out, Marks & Spencer dress on, feeling good, looking alright. We get into the club and about an hour and a half into the night, I decide to get on the dancefloor as they were playing one of my favourite songs. Not dancing with anyone in particular, I start going all in, arms and legs akimbo, throwing some shapes on the dancefloor and twerking up a storm. I'm feeling great! All eyes were on me and for the first time in a long time, I felt somewhat free and normal.

That was until I went back to join my friends and have a quick drink.

I turned around to order another drink and all I hear from behind me is, 'STEPH.AN.IE, WOZZDAT?'

I turned around and looked at my friend in confusion. I slowly followed her shocked gaze to my back, but couldn't see why she was so confused. I ignored her and continued to order my drink.

About a minute later, I feel a hand grab my wrist and pull me from the bar, to the bathroom.

Once in the bathroom, my mate starts screaming with laughter and asks me to look at my butt in the long length mirror.

Guys, I felt a big, old sweat of terror drip down my face before I turned around, because somehow I just knew that it had something to do with my favourite undergarments.

I slowly turned around and to my horror...one chicken fillet (which was beige in colour btw) was dangling under my dress by the skin of its teeth. The other chicken fillet had ridden up my back, making it look like I had some kind of huge growth on my spine.

I truly wanted the earth to swallow me whole. I had never been more embarrassed than in that moment. I quickly ran into a bathroom stall to take the fillets out and stuff them down my bra, then came out, burst out laughing and pretended like I was fine with the whole situation; that it was just 'BANTER'. Deep down, I wanted to die.

That was the last time I used the pads, as I couldn't risk something like that happening again. Funny story, right? But at the time, I didn't find it funny at all. The world (the four friends I was out with that night and a couple of drunk ladies in the loo) had found out my secret – that I wasn't naturally hourglass shaped with a blessed behind – and now I felt like a fraud.

Over the years, I'd go on to try several things in order to attain the glorified 'black female shape' – I went back to doing weights again, I attended a couple of consultations with doctors about the prospect of having surgery – although at the time, butt lifts and butt fat transfers were so rare in

the UK, so any likelihood of my butt turning out somewhat great would have been a rare one.

A few years ago, I came across this phenomena on YouTube called the Chicken Pill, a pill that – allegedly – could increase not only your breast size, but your butt size too. I was obsessed.

The 'chicken pills' in question were actually hormone pills, the same hormones that farmers gave to chickens to make them grow at an expeditious rate.

Somehow, these pills had been modified for consumption by humans, and were now making their way online for purchase. I was at a point in my life where my personal health and safety was at an all-round low for me, and so, still in the interests of pursuing this ideal body, I purchased some of the pills.

Safe to say, I didn't last too long on them before I started throwing up and feeling incredibly ill. I didn't see changes to my body, and £55 had gone down the drain.

You can't force it, babe

A simple subheading, but it really is what it is. Non-conformity is a strong theme running within this book, but it's absolutely true – absolutely no one should feel the pressure to conform to what is essentially, a damaging stereotype exacerbated by patriarchal standards! Do womxn with these body shapes receive more attention? Of course they do, but it doesn't – and shouldn't – make us feel any less of a person because we don't have those attributes. I have a flat butt (in my opinion) and a wide waist. My top half is also much bigger than my bottom half, which means my body type is almost like an inverted triangle of sorts. I hated it. I wished that my body could swap around, with the heaviest part of me being on the bottom as opposed to the top.

When I entered my first relationship, I would be lying if I said my mind wasn't slightly blown by the fact that someone actually 'allegedly' found me attractive. This person had a penchant for curvier womxn, so I'd be lying if I said that during the early stages of the relationship, I didn't try and make myself smaller (whilst trying to make the 'right' sides of me bigger) in a bid to try and appear more attractive, and more acceptable. Although I was generally happy, I couldn't help but be mega aware that the person I was with had a preference for curvier, black womxn and although I had been 'chosen', I still didn't feel that I fit the right 'type' of fat.

When undergoing the break-up a couple of years later, I actually ended up losing a significant amount of weight due to heartbreak and depression completely robbing me of my appetite. I remember one day taking a mirror selfie, and noticing that my arse looked HUGE, because of the weight that I had lost around my back/middle. I was HYPED I have to admit. I'd never seen anything like it and for a split second, a part of me wished I could have stayed this shape forever.

Eventually the weight came back as my appetite returned and when it did, it really forced me to think about my position as someone who preaches about self-love, yet still heralded a specific body type as the 'supreme'. Not for 'society' in general, no. But because men liked it. I had to sit with myself for a while and ask myself why

I was so hell bent on receiving validation from men, when (for the most part) all they do is go around causing drama and heartache, LOL?!

So, for me, it spoke to a deeper issue about how I viewed myself and my body. Although I was lightyears ahead in confidence, it was clear that there were some self-esteem issues and a bulk of un-learning that still had to be done.

And that my friends, is the short tale of how I tried to change my body in order to feel more African.

It's weird isn't it? The things we sometimes do in order to feel like we have to fit in. Today, more and more womxn are undertaking BBL and hip surgery in order to look like their favourite female rappers and Instagram stars. The hourglass shape is officially in, and I can't see it going anytime soon. It's not only white womxn such as Kim and Khloe Kardashian who are going after these body shapes (in a bid to attain a more 'ethnic' body shape used to attract black men in my opinion), but it's black womxn who are also desiring the extreme, exaggerated body shape, and why wouldn't they? The stereotypical 'black female shape' has been celebrated, fetishized, and desired within our communities for hundreds of years.

These days, we are hearing more and more in the press about the womxn who are killing themselves (literally) in the quest to have the perfect hourglass-shaped body, complete with big booty. Brazilian butt lifts are big business, especially in European countries where they are often cheaper (or even free, if you have a decent enough Instagram following), and flocks of black womxn are heading overseas to undertake these risky procedures.

In 2018, it was reported that a second womxn, Leah Cambridge, 29, had died from having a Brazilian Butt Lift procedure, suffering from three heart attacks while under anaesthetic. Leah was reportedly unhappy with her body shape after having three children and wanted to re-shape her stomach and bum. In the same vein, 24-year-old Joy Williams from London sadly passed away after her wounds became infected after having surgery in Bangkok in 2014[9].

9 https://www.bbc.co.uk/news/av/uk-england-london-29791057/cosmetic-surgery-warning-follows-joy-williams-death

The British Association of Aesthetic Plastic Surgeons (BAAPS) calls it the most dangerous cosmetic procedure to undergo (with as high as 1 in 3000 deaths being reported)[10], because of the high risk of blood clotting and cardiac arrest due to the super important nerve endings and vessels that are located within that area. Knowing this, scores of womxn still choose to fly out to undertake this life-threatening surgery. I have – on many occasions – considered having the procedure due to the pressure I felt I was under to look a specific way, especially on Instagram.

It's not something I think I would ever do as I'm an absolute COWARD when it comes to surgery and being put to sleep, but there are days when I do fantasize about having a huge, round posterior. At the end of the day, even though most surgeries carry the risk of potential death, is even the slightest risk of death worth it?

The pressure on black womxn to have the 'supposed shape of a black womxn' is absolutely crippling; and if you're plus-size, there's this automatic assumption that the 'more' body you have, the more your fat will be stored in the 'right' places, i.e., our butts and our breasts, but fat doesn't work like that. Fat will store itself wherever it damn well pleases on our body, and we can try and manipulate and shift it to where we think it would look the most attractive but at the end of the day, it isn't going anywhere. I spoke to a couple of my black, plus-size followers on Twitter to pick their brain on whether they had ever considered having an augmentation:

---

10 https://baaps.org.uk/media/press_releases/1630/the_bottom_line

'I've definitely felt like I wasn't living up to the ideal by having a flat ass.'

'Both my sister and Mum have been blessed with THEE buttocks and I have the big boobs. Which can be a blessing but mostly a curse and when people see the front, they generally assume the back matches. It's definitely an insecurity of mine and I'm in the process of trying to get some squats in regularly. The reason why I wanted it was mainly because of the stereotype – I've been told that I don't have a black girl's bum – and my mum and sister have both poked fun at me. I don't want an outrageous bottom but one that definitely suits my body being plus-sized and not having one seems wrong in a way.'
– @Lesley_Louiise

'I've definitely felt like I wasn't living up to the ideal by having a flat ass. I think that hourglass shapes are privileged and with the accessibility and visibility of plastic surgery, obtaining an hourglass shape has always felt so attainable and also far-fetched at the same time due to financial constraints and the fact that they don't really operate on plus-size patients. I've always wanted a fat ass tho.'
– @BadFatBlackGirl

'Only fairly recently did I start to despise and begrudge my body shape. The trigger was my last and my first boyfriend. During the relationship he would point out other womxn with a bigger bum and say "We're gonna get you like that". I remember his exact words because it shocked me so much. I also remember when he grabbed my back roll in public and said it was unacceptable for me to have fat. He would also point out and make fun of how small my bum is considering the rest of me and say "it doesn't make sense". He cheated on me with a girl who was also overweight but had a significantly bigger bum. He'd also talk about how it was "in my genes" to have a big bum and a small waist, because I'm black. We broke up, needless to say.

I used to spend hours every day watching BBL vlogs, surgeries and before and afters. It got to a point where out of 500 people I followed on Instagram, more than half were BBL patients or surgeons. It was very unhealthy for me to consume that sort of content every day. I also started comparing myself to white womxn on a daily basis which I think made me really bitter.'
– @BadBlackBruja

Of course, we also know that a lot of these societal pressures also stem from – you guessed it – the *patriarchy* *shakes fist*. Men seem to have very strong ideas about what the ideal black body should be like. Not just black men, no! All races too. When I found out that my ex had broken up with me because he wanted someone with a more 'hourglass' shape (which included the small waist/big bum combo – yes I did ask him for details, self-sabotage innit), I was absolutely dumbfounded. Not because his reasons were absolutely shit and shallow to begin with, but because he too, had imposed his own impressions of what the stereotypical 'black body' should look like, and looking back, it was almost fetishistic in its approach. What a dick.

As with a lot of body politics surrounding black womxn, a lot of this can be traced back to the fetishism of the black, female body like I discussed in previous chapters.

The age of the 'music video vixen' in hip hop videos also did nothing to curb this obsession with having acceptable curves. I grew up idolising these womxn and praying that one day, the puppy fat would just drop off and I would be reborn into a body like the ones I saw on TV. I know this sounds cliché AF but at the end of the day, we are so much more than the ideologies and the expectations put on us by men. When you really have a sit down and think about WHY you want a specific figure, and eventually realize it's because men set the standard (and we all know that men perpetually move mad), it can really help as a catalyst towards shedding all the patriarchal toxic behaviour and thoughts that have been ingrained in us since childhood.

Let our bodies just 'be' bodies!

Whether you are slim or fat, tall or short, black, Asian, Latina, Middle Eastern, white or mixed race, it's important to acknowledge that there is absolutely no such thing as 'The Perfect Body' and growing up, we have never had a realistic expectation of what an ideal body should be. Why? Because body shapes appear to us in the form of 'trends'. What is deemed as beautiful RIGHT NOW? Which brands and companies can make money off of our fleeting insecurities? How many new clients can plastic surgeons get in the next 10 years? From the heroin chic phase of the Nineties, to the lithe, athletic phase of the Eighties, to the current Kardashian body craze, we've been taught as womxn to never feel at home with our bodies and to see our bodies as spare parts, to be replaced every six years or so. Our bodies shouldn't be trends: we should be allowed to just...be.

Body types shouldn't have to come in and out of fashion, and just because my body or yours isn't what is currently seen as the accepted trend, it doesn't mean that we should wait around until it is. It's not your job to be beautiful, and when you stop equating the ideal body with happiness, it is so much easier to love yourself completely!

Beauty does not align with happiness, friends, love, etc. Being a size 10, having an absolutely MASSIVE butt, or having the desired hourglass shape will not make your life happier. You were made to do whatever you want with whatever body you have, so it's important not to focus on other peoples' bodies, because at the end of the day the only one you have is your own. Just try existing in this amazing, marvellous, unique, splendiferous, miraculous, sexy, gorgeous body you were born in. You are in competition with absolutely NO ONE.

So, NO! Just because I am FAT, does not mean that I have to have big boobs, a big bum, or a small waist in order to 'pass' as attractive.

Just because I'm black, does NOT mean I have to have the body shape expected of me. My blackness is not invalidated because I lack a butt, or big hips and a small waist. Our beauty is non-conforming, and we should be able to celebrate our curves in, however, they choose to present themselves – hourglass, pear, apple, rectangle, bin bag shaped, or not.

SHAKES FIST AT SIR MIX-A-LOT AND HIS INVOLVEMENT IN IMPLEMENTING THE DESIRED '36-24-36' BODY MEASUREMENT AMONGST BLACK WOMXN!

135

36-24-36? In This Economy?!

BINGO TIME

THE CURVE ILLUSION BINGO!

If I were to define my body type, I think I'd say it most likely fits the inverted triangle, but growing up, it didn't stop me from near enough breaking my back in order to get those #angles to give the illusion of desirable curves and a butt! I feel like we've all been there in some way, shape or form, so take a look at the bingo sheet opposite, and have a drink every time you see a statement that resonates with you (or cross a statement off if you're not doing the rum tonight!).

BINGO

Taken a mirror selfie in your bathroom while carefully angling your butt on the bath/sink so it looks girthy and swole.	Taken a selfie arching/twisting your back out while wearing a pair of gym leggings.	Worn a corset underneath clothing to achieve desired hourglass shape.
Worn/bought butt pads to achieve desired hourglass shape.	Used an app to slightly 'enhance' your features, but forgot that the wall pattern was also bending and warping with your shape.	Asked a friend to take a poolside snap with you sitting on the edge of the pool wearing a high rise bikini – arse cheeks spread apart – to give the illusion of a bigger bum.
Taken out a £70 gym membership to carry out target weightloss around your waist, only to find out that you cannot lose weight in target areas =/.	Worn two corsets on top of each other for the desired effect when you go out, only to flinch and move away whenever anyone comes in contact with you, lest they accidentally graze the boning and wiring underneath your outfit and figure out the jig is up.	Accidently broken said sink in the first statement by leaning too much on it in order to take the perfect selfie.

Why Do You Want That Body? A Reason Tree

One exercise that has really helped me process my thoughts and feelings about how and why I wanted to look a particular way was to create a 'reason tree'. A pretty simple, yet effective concept; I simply write a statement that I 'think' I believe in, and ask myself why. When I have answered the question, I ask myself why again, until I get down to the root of the matter. It's something that I learned during therapy, and anytime I'm in a situation where I doubt myself or have a lack of belief in myself, I draw up my little reason tree to try and get down to the real issues.

Opposite, I have sketched out a little reason tree for you to answer, for those who are still in the mindset that they need to look a specific way or have a specific body shape. Have a little read and answer as much or as little as you feel comfortable doing. The intended result is that you come to realize that all your negative fears and doubts are based on outside factors whose opinions and ideologies bear no importance on who you are as a person!

What is the
ideal body shape
I want?

Why do I want
to have this specific
body shape?

What will
I gain by being
this body shape?

What is wrong
with the body shape
I have now?

Who has told me that
this specific body
shape is desirable?

Why have I decided
that the opinions and
ideologies of this specific
demographic (mostly
men innit? Let's be
honest, LMAO) are more
important than how I feel
about myself?

Do I hold the
opinions of others
above my own?

Am I wanting to
change my body
shape to please them
or to please myself?

If there were no such
thing as standards
of beauty, would I be
happy in the body I'm
in? Does it get me from
A to B? Can I rely on it?

Am I confident
in my identity?

Why am I allowing
the opinions of others
to tamper with my
self-esteem?

Do I love
myself?

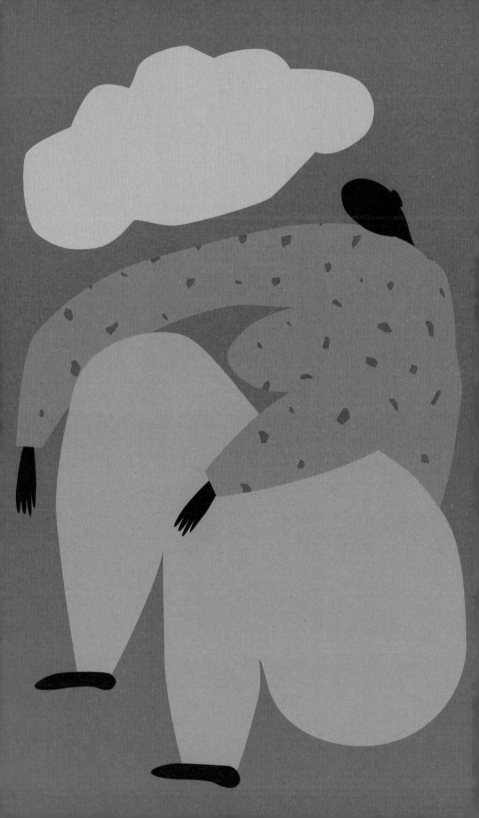

Chapter
SIX

This Fat Body Has Been Complicit In Breaking My Brain!

Highlighting the mental health effects of being plus-size is something that I definitely thought should be spoken about in this book, as mental health is the fabric that weaves all the other elements together. You cannot talk about one element of fatness, fatphobia, racism associated with fatphobia, or societal pressures without mentioning mental health and the negative impact it can have on us.

What is this weird feeling in my brain?!

Before we get started, a quick disclaimer here that I will be chatting about issues from when I was diagnosed with clinical depression at age 14.

A fact not a lot of people know; in fact, I went to extraordinary lengths to hide this from people, not that I had many people around me at the time to hide it from. As mentioned in a previous chapter, my body image issues didn't really kick in until I started secondary school, and even then, I didn't really notice that a storm was brewing in my head until it was too late. I pretty much did the typical things a tween/teenager would do when put under intense stress and fear due to bullying; I would shut myself away for hours on end and cry, I would isolate myself, listen to sad songs on the radio, eat excessively, compare myself to the beautiful celebrities I would see in magazines and on TV, and would generally just be very quiet and very full of #teen #angst.

I began noticing little subtle changes, however.

I began imagining what my life would be like if I, A: wasn't here anymore, or B: were smaller. They weren't just subtle daydreams, however, they were incredibly intense visions of alternate universes I had created for myself. On the days where I would be getting bullied rather intensely, I would completely shut down and enter into this amazing new alternate universe. A universe where I was lighter-skinned, slim, and had loads of friends. I would create secondary characters in this play and would often communicate with them out loud (all the while being very aware that I was talking to myself). This continued until quite recently, when I eventually found out that what I was doing was something called 'disassociation', a technique our brains do in order to process trauma and self-soothe. Not only would I frequently disassociate, but I would also begin to self-harm by way of pulling out my eyebrow hair frequently and also taking a pair of scissors and slicing it across my tummy, because I wanted to cut it off so badly. Obviously at the time, I didn't see what I was doing as destructive behaviour; I saw it more as me repairing a problem.

As I got older, the self-hate and insecurity over how I looked became all-consuming. After school, I would frequently just lie in bed in the dark, just staring at the ceiling and crying, or I would be online trying to research how to lose weight and in a very short space of time. I was on Weight Watchers at the time too, so my eating became incredibly disordered – something I will touch on a bit later.

I didn't formally recognize my descent into depression until I noticed that I no longer found the things I had previously found fun, to be fun anymore. I was an avid reader and I absolutely LOVED to sing. I noticed that I'd gradually stopped doing this and instead, would take to mindlessly staring at the TV, not talking anymore. It felt like it was a huge chore to just wake up every day, and I would navigate the days with a huge pain in my chest.

Thoughts of ending my life weren't new to me, and as the bullying began to get more and more intense, I started to have those thoughts often; how I would do it, when I would do it, and would anyone miss me? I would also draw up lists of why I thought I didn't deserve to be here and surprise, surprise, the large majority of the lists often featured things to do with my body, or the idea of being desirable/wanted.

It was somewhat of a covert mission to see my GP (on the recommendation of my school counsellor) for an appointment, as I was still underage, but somehow I was able to get the appointment and talk through my issues. A little while later, I started attending therapy, although it didn't last long as I wasn't used to opening up and chatting about how I felt. All I knew was that my body was the cause of all the misfortunes in my life. Being born in a body that coped with such a huge amount of external hate and negativity grinded my gears, and I just wanted it all to stop.

I also feel like a large part of my depression and the way I felt about my body stemmed from how I felt I was seen by my family while existing in this fat body. Mental health is an issue that to this day is still seen as somewhat of a taboo subject within the Afro-Caribbean and African American communities. Even though studies have shown the increasing rate in mental health illnesses within black men and womxn (often surpassing other races of late)[II], the subject of discussing mental health within our communities is still seen as wrong. At home, I often felt like I couldn't talk about the weird, sad things happening in my brain – not just because I was shy and a bit of a wallflower – but for fear that I wouldn't be believed. In our culture (speaking generally here), depression and anxiety aren't classed as 'real things'. For the most part, I feel as if they are typically seen as just having 'bad days', thus we are expected to get over these feelings as soon as possible.

From what I can remember, I was always very close with my dad as a young child. As the first born, I was spoiled with the nicest clothes and the latest toys, and all was pretty good in the hood. This relationship changed as I started to get older – and coincidentally – bigger.

145

II   https://www.mentalhealth.org.uk/a-to-z/b/black-asian-and-minority-ethnic-bame-communities

I noticed that my dad began to pick on my size constantly, as well as become a lot harsher on me even though I was a good kid, and so I spent a large part of my childhood and early teenhood confused by this, yet unable to challenge or question him as to why, due to being slightly intimidated by him.

Alongside being bullied about my weight in school, I would then have to come home, and be subjected to unsolicited fat-shamey comments about my weight from him too. It was almost like he was ashamed of me for putting on weight and would lecture myself and my mum about how I looked, and how my weight may have a hand in setting me back in life. When eating, he would snatch the plate away from me if I was eating too much. He would often call me lazy and would compare me to other people. In all honesty...it felt like he really withdrew the 'love' aspect of our relationship when I started putting on weight, and it's something that I've never really wanted to explore until now. It's definitely had an impact on my mental health, in a sense that as body positive and confident as I am today, there is still a small part of me that reverts back to 'pre-pubescent, insecure, 'wanting-her-Father's-approval' Steph whenever it comes to the subject of men and their approval of me and my body. Weird innit?

Fat people get eating disorders too

Fast forward a few years until I reached the age of about 22. As I swallowed yet another generic diet pill (pills I had been given by an extended family member of mine, and washed it down with orange juice, of course, to help the pill absorb better), my mind wandered to the influx of outfits and on-trend pieces I would eventually be able to fit into, and all the attention that I would eventually start receiving from the opposite sex once the rest of the weight ultimately dropped off. By this point, I had lost four stone and was in a hotel bathroom in Barcelona for my 23rd birthday. People around me were congratulating me for losing weight and it felt so, so good.

I carried out my daily morning heave, which had become something of a ritual at this point, popped on my bikini, and hit the beach.

This routine of bulimia combined with extreme food deprivation was a habit I learned from being made to attend a dieting membership club as a young teenager. There, I was taught to consume as few calories as possible (sometimes surviving on up to only 600 calories a day), and I was congratulated on losing weight, with no one questioning my methods of doing so.

Each day consisted of me pre-weighing my cereal and milk before school, weighing my lunch to make sure it added up to the 350 calorie recommendation, cheating during lunch and having a Mars Bar, then throwing everything up afterwards in a bid to keep within my calorie goal in time for weigh-in at the next dieters' meeting.

The dieting programme definitely taught me extreme restrictive eating habits. I walked away with a binge eating disorder that went undetected for many years, in part because, for the longest time, I didn't think I had one. When I did bring up the possibility of having an eating disorder, no one understood or believed me, and thus it caused me to question if I really did have one.

Approximately 1.25 million people in the United Kingdom have an eating disorder, according to the Beat Eating Disorders charity[12]. And guess what? Some of them are fat, too. Over the years, a disturbing misconception has appeared, fuelled by the media, that in order to be suffering from an eating disorder, you must fit into an ideal body shape. When people think of 'eating disorders', they normally visualize images of slim womxn starving themselves or forcing themselves to throw up. Images show visible rib cages, 'lollipop heads[13]', and protruding spines, but this was certainly not the case with me, and many, many other plus-size people all over the world who have eating disorders.

I feel that most marginalized bodies, with the exception of cisgender womxn, are thought not to be affected by eating disorders. But the ugly truth is that eating disorders

147

---

12 https://www.beateatingdisorders.org.uk/media-centre/eating-disorder-statistics
13 https://www.foxnews.com/story/lollipop-head-starlets-start-fashion-trend

affect people of all ages, races, genders, abilities, ethnicities, socioeconomic status, and body shapes.

Many people still see the idea of a fat person who stops eating as someone who is 'doing the right thing for their health', and our cultural view of fatness as inherently unhealthy plays heavily into that. Even now, I can anticipate the scores of people who will tell me that you can't actually be anorexic if you are clinically 'overweight' or 'obese', since the clinical criteria for Anorexia Nervosa historically requires you to be medically underweight[14].

BUT THE GAG IS...research has actually shown that medical professionals often miss eating disorders in overweight teens because of these inherent anti-fat biases[15]. But I also know I'm far from the only fat womxn to suffer from an eating disorder, and it's time for people to see that bulimia and other similar disorders can affect more than just thin womxn.

I didn't acknowledge my disorder until I was halfway through my self-love journey while seeing a therapist, who would question me on particular details on how I coped with bullying, such as eating, self-harm, and other things of that nature. It was only when I described to her the many complexities of my eating habits that she made me aware of the serious issue I had surrounding my relationship with food. To this day, I still eat specific foods in a certain order, and even though I prefer to leave the meat and fish last on my plate like a lot of other people, my reasoning for doing this is to hope that I am full enough by the time I get to the meat, so I won't have to eat it.

Our cultural obsession with thinness and cisgender-normative beauty standards are deeply harmful to the psyches of all womxn, but particularly to fat womxn and to an extent, fat womxn of colour (again under the assumption that black, fat womxn are happier in our bodies due to it being a 'preference' within our communities – remember, this is a scam!).

Our bodies are beautiful and worthy of love just as they are, despite the ugly messages that are continually dumped all over them. And those of us who have struggled

14 https://www.eatingdisorder.org/eating-disorder-information/
    anorexia-nervosa/
15 https://consent.yahoo.com/collectConsent?sessionId=3_cc-session
    _65ae0b15-9c32-4c65-bd8b-007c2a5015f2&lang=en-gb&inline=false

with that, and have been through real and legitimate eating disorders, deserve to have our experiences acknowledged for what they are.

We must work harder to include more diverse narratives. Fat people can, and do, have eating disorders. Including them and allowing them to feel comfortable openly expressing their thoughts and experiences with illnesses such as anorexia and bulimia, could make it easier for them to cope and recover.

I want to leave this little section with a message to anyone reading this who has felt like no one would believe that they are struggling with an eating disorder. Please reach out! Your experiences are valid and important. You are important. Never stop trying and remember there are so many communities waiting for you with open arms to offer support.

Mental health and weight

Now, remember a few paragraphs ago when I mentioned my eating disorder and my absolute desperation to lose weight as quickly as possible? Well, after I came back from Barcelona, all the weight piled back on with HASTE. That's something that a lot of these diet gurus and magazines fail to tell you in their relentlessness to push diet culture onto society and earn the big bucks: if you try and lose weight from a place of self-hate, you absolutely will put the weight back on, or will be violently ill. Now this chapter isn't about weightloss or me telling you the best ways to lose weight, but in circumstances where you find yourself wanting to lose weight for whatever reason, it's imperative that you are able to do it from a place of love. You have to come from a place of loving your body enough to want good things for it, and to look after it every step of the way.

If you approach weightloss from a place of shame and self-hate, your brain will be trying to lose weight as quickly as possible in order to move away from the image it sees and hates in the mirror every day. This means that you'll automatically want to lose weight as quickly as possible. Nothing good has ever come from losing weight as quickly as possible because for the most part, a lot of people will take to extremes such as starvation,

'We've been conditioned as children to see bigger people as the villains from the types of content we were exposed to growing up.'

weightloss pills, 'detoxing', and other dangerous methods in order to lose the weight fast.

The thing that really bugs me sometimes when we talk about weight and mental health, is that when you go online and google the search terms 'weight + mental health', or 'plus-size + depression', you'll find a million and one articles which discuss weight gain as the primary cause of depression, or obesity being a mental health trigger. Outside of personal blog posts and first-person opinion pieces surrounding mental health, you rarely see articles about mental health and weight where our weight isn't placed as the 'bad guy' or the 'cause'. Rarely do these articles talk about the sociological factors that are linked with weight and mental health. Our weight is always seen as the 'problem', as opposed to people's attitudes and treatment towards our weight. The onus is on us to change how we look – thus feeding into the ideology that fatness is inherently an 'us' problem, and that in order to fit in with the rest of society and avoid being harrassed, bullied, or policed, we have to change our bodies. It's of vital importance that the way in which we are treated by society based on our body types is addressed also. The onus should be on the aggressors to change (this includes individuals, the media, and companies) their mindset towards different body types.

I've spoken in previous chapters about the way in which the media could help change people's attitudes towards fat people, and that is by portraying fat people as human beings, as opposed to freak shows. Not only does this apply to reality shows, the news, documentaries, and sitcoms, but also cartoons! We've been conditioned as children to see bigger people as the villains from the types of content we were exposed to growing up. From Disney villians (Ursula the Sea Witch in The Little Mermaid, the Queen of Hearts in Alice in Wonderland, and Governor Ratcliffe in Pocahontas, among many others) to the roster of oversized alien villains in Dr Who, and The Penguin in Batman, the message is clear: fat = bad.

In fact, I've only been able to find one study so far, and that was undertaken by the University of Exeter and the University of South Australia[16], who examined more than 48,000 people and found that the 'psychological

---

16 https://www.exeter.ac.uk/news/featurednews/title_691796_en.html

impact of being obese is likely to cause depression'. The suggestion is that the 'health issues' that can stem from being fat isn't the main cause of depression – in other words, choosing to have a Big Mac with chicken nuggets and an apple pie isn't going to be the cause of your depression and anxiety in most cases. Being fat and having clinical sadness do not feed off each other in self-destructive slivers. It is the mental impact of being plus-size that is the problem.

It just seems like such a logical answer doesn't it? It's amazing that there aren't more studies about it if I'm being honest, but yes, judgment of people who are overweight absolutely definitely does contribute to the disintegration of one's self-esteem and mental health. GROUNDBREAKING I KNOW, RIGHT?

So if you're someone with a 'healthy' BMI (even though we now know that the whole notion of BMI is complete bollocks) and you're randomly complaining about feeling 'fat' in front of someone who is actually visibly fat (who's now realising that you see their body as lesser/unattractive), you're 'technically' a public health hazard, LOL! You are the mental equivalent of eating 100 bananas a day – at first you think it's good, healthy even – but you're slowly poisoning yourself and others around you (although I'm not sure if potassium is airborne enough to be 'caught' from others, but you GET MY ANALOGY AND THAT'S THE MOST IMPORTANT THING). Essentially, you're poisoning the mental wellbeing of those around you.

Equally, let's say that you work in Hollywood and you're producing a film that stars a plus-size lead who sustains a very serious head injury (the plot line of movies *I Feel Pretty* and *Isn't it Romantic*) in order to be confident enough to have a successful romantic life, to be loved, and feel as if her beauty is on par with the standard societal standards of beauty; and those watching are invited to laugh at the sheer 'ridiculousness' of an overweight womxn believing she's worthy of love. If you're involved in those films, you could possibly – or maybe even probably – be contributing to an environment that negatively affects the mental health and wellbeing of your audience. Maybe your film poster should contain a trigger warning?

Or what about that 'well meaning' charity or the government-funded campaigns to fight obesity in the

UK? Making my way into town, I would see multiple billboards at every train station and high street with the words 'OBESITY' emblazoned in bold, aggressive looking font, carrying such an air of judgement and disgust. This is something I will touch on more in the next chapter, but those campaigns that have been proven time and time again to not be as effective as they think, could be seen as detrimental to one's mental health too. Is the impulse to help enough to justify the negative impact; the buzz all this adds to the white noise of negativity that fat people are surrounded by already?

Fat-shaming is shit...Stop it!

As well-intentioned and as 'harmless' as your movie or your random musings about your weight may claim to be, they all still fall under the category of fat-shaming, e.g., the last acceptable form of hate crime. I call it so, as the vast majority of abuse, harassment, and policing is hidden in plain sight, through advertising, through unsolicited messages of 'concern' from health trolls, from friends and family alike, and from the health industry. The insidious way in which this prejudice has been able to insert itself so neatly and effortlessly into our society is almost brilliant, if it wasn't so unbelievably cruel.

As we'll go on to see in the next chapter, there is a weird part of society who believe that making fat people feel ashamed of their weight or eating habits may motivate them to lose weight. Equally, there is scientific evidence that confirms that nothing could be further from the truth. Science tells us a lot of things that people are incredibly quick to believe, because ya' know...science. But let science tell you that behaving like a dickhead to people who look different, is damaging, and then all of a sudden, they can't read. DISGUSTEN.

We've seen time and time again that instead of motivating people, fat-shaming just makes us feel terrible about ourselves, which in turn can affect our mental health, that can – in some instances – cause us to eat even more, thus putting on more weight (not that THAT would be anyone's business either!). If you've come this far into the book and are still confused as to what fat-shaming is exactly, allow me to define it for you:

'The message
is clear –
fat = bad.'

Fat-shaming essentially involves criticizing and harassing fat people about their weight or their eating habits in order to make them feel ashamed of themselves.

People who undertake this sordid practice believe that by being horrible to fat people, it may encourage us to 'eat healthier and exercise more' – in order to fit in with the current Westernized aesthetic ideals of beauty. In the majority of cases, the people who are at the helm of fat-shaming are smaller and have never had to live in a plus-size body.

There is also research that shows that much of the discussion on fatness – especially on social media – involves fat-shaming, which in turn can turn into harassment and cyberbullying – especially against womxn.[17]

In the 12 years of having a presence online, I can easily say that about 70 per cent of the interaction I get from people online is of an abusive, fat-shaming nature. I have message boards dedicated to me, who blame my weight, my race, and my hyperpigmentation for not being able to find love or be treated with the basic common decency and respect I deserve as a human being. I understand that putting myself out there will no doubt attract opinions in all its forms, but it doesn't make the results any less cutting. I also know that these things happen to plus-size womxn all the time, across the board. Being online as a fat can be annoying at the best of times.

As well as the mental health issues, fat-shaming can ALSO cause stress, which we all know is one of the biggest killers. It can raise cortisol levels, which can turn can leave someone open to a host of other diseases. Some of you may think that this shouldn't be considered harmful, abusive, or cruel. You may personally not think that they could have a hand in causing depression. But the research suggests that they actually may. Eventually, something needs to change. We need to be kinder to each other, to put it simply. And should it really take a medical research study for us to consider that idea?

This Fat Body Has Been Complicit In Breaking My Brain!

---

17   https://www.ncbi.nlm.nih.gov/pmc/articles/PMC4167901/

Eating disorders look different on Black women and the conversation is wildly different when it comes to us. Period.

100% of the programs i've ever seen on TV about eating disorders have all been about white women. I can't recall one single story where the subject was anorexia and a black person was included. Let me know if thats just me tho.

156   Black, fat womxn get eating disorders too

Case in point, along with my example from a few pages ago, to highlight that normally when we think about eating disorders, we picture a slim white womxn with a visible rib cage and a gaunt face. Even when it comes to mental health and eating disorders, white womxn are still the standard. This is partly the reason why so many black womxn find it difficult to come forward about eating disorders – that, and the fact that sometimes, being from an Afro-Caribbean or African American culture sometimes doesn't provide the safe atmosphere one would need and hope for, in order to share something so vulnerable and personal. Lemme throw a couple of US-based stats at you:

* Black teenagers are 50% times more likely than white teenagers to exhibit bulimic behaviour, such as binging and purging.[18]

* People of colour with self-acknowledged eating and weight concerns were significantly less likely than white participants to have been asked by a doctor about eating disorder symptoms, despite similar rates of eating disorder symptoms across ethnic groups.[19]

* When presented with identical case studies demonstrating disordered eating symptoms in white, Hispanic, and black womxn, clinicians were asked to identify if the womxn's eating behaviour was problematic; 44% identified the white womxn's behaviour as problematic; 41% identified the Hispanic womxn's behaviour as problematic, and only 17% identified the black womxn's behaviour as problematic. The clinicians were also less likely to recommend that the black womxn should receive professional help.[20] (Author's note: OMFG?!).

There can be a couple of explanations for this. Eating disorders in black womxn and womxn of colour may be, in part, a response to environmental stress (i.e., abuse, racism, poverty). Therefore, given the multiple traumas that we can be exposed to, we may be more vulnerable to eating disorders than our white counterparts.

The third statistic is the one that really troubled me, to be honest. There has long been this myth within the healthcare industry that black womxn are physically 'stronger' and more equipped to handle pain than our white counterparts. This also goes for mental/emotional issues too. Therefore, because of this, we aren't given the same level or duty of care as white womxn. We've recently heard statistics being thrown about this year that back up this theory, such as black womxn in the UK being five times more likely to die in childbirth[21] than white womxn due to lack of care and racial microaggressions (with

18 Goeree, Sovinsky, & Iorio, 2011
19 Becker, 2003
20 Gordon, Brattole, Wingate, & Joiner, 2006
21 https://www.bbc.co.uk/news/av/stories-49607727/black-womxn-five-times-more-likely-to-die-in-childbirth

African American womxn three times more likely to die during childbirth than white womxn[22]), and the same can be said for how we deal with emotional trauma too.

So, bringing it back to black bodies, disordered eating, and the lack of visibility, I'll say this: lifelong battles with multiple sets of beauty standards leave many black womxn with no choice but to engage in disordered eating in an effort to almost...'correct' our 'fundamentally flawed' bodies.

Black womxn as a whole, are expected to live up to these conflicting beauty standards, which result in strained relationships with ourselves, our bodies, and our food. And at the core of disordered eating is a fundamental dissatisfaction with food that results in eating too much or too little of it, usually as a way to 'correct' weight and shape, but also as a way to regain control or even process emotions that one is not allowed to properly feel or voice in the correct way. I know *so many* black girls who have struggled[23] with this in some way, shape or form, and even their mothers before them, who may then project these ideologies and habits onto them. Yet we are casually omitted from larger mainstream conversations about eating disorders, mostly because our purported 'strength' dictates that we should be immune[24] to 'weak' diseases like eating disorders. That suffering from an eating disorder is a 'white girl' illness[25]. And that any discomfort we display with food or our bodies is a personal failing rather than a tragic display of a world that hates our bodies yet takes what it wants from us, time and time again.

Furthermore, in 2017, a study conducted on college campuses in the United States found clear discriminatory practices among health professionals when acknowledging, diagnosing and treating eating disorders in young black womxn versus their white counterparts.[26] Obviously influenced by the stereotype of the 'strong black womxn' (*groan*), doctors in the

---

22 https://www.nbcnews.com/news/nbcblk/us-pregnancy-deaths-are-especially-among-black-women-n1003806
23 https://www.thedailybeast.com/black-women-suffer-from-eating-disorders-too
24 https://scholars.org/contribution/how-expectation-strength-harms-black-girls-and-women
25 https://www.huffpost.com/entry/opinion-yarrow-eating-disorders-white-women_n_5a945db3e4b0699553cb1d00
26 https://uncjourney.unc.edu/files/2017/05/JOURneySpring2017vol1Digital.pdf

study appeared not to believe that black womxn were susceptible to disordered eating. One of the professionals interviewed for the study, who worked in counselling and psychological services at a largely-white Southern school, said she wasn't aware of recent research on disordered eating in non-white womxn. Can you imagine? This person, who allegedly specialized in eating disorders, said she'd heard 'talk in the past that non-white womxn had different perspectives on what was acceptable in terms of body shape and size,' but she didn't know if 'that theory has already been debunked'.

Stories like these, together with the general distrust of medical professionals that many black people feel[27], can discourage black people with eating disorders from seeking help.

For me, I never really sought help for what I was going through, as in my mind, I thought it was what I deserved. My punishment for being so fat. Punishment for not looking the way 'normal' black womxn are 'supposed' to look. I obviously couldn't tell my family either, because I assumed that they would either ignore it, or laugh it off. I felt like from their point of view, it would be absurd to claim to have an eating disorder because of all the hungry people back home in Ghana who weren't afforded the privilege to have free access to food like I was. There was an inherent cultural shame knowing that I came from a country positioned in a 'third world' continent (for the most part) and yet I was choosing to not eat food, while people starved.

It taught me that even in the midst of our mental health struggles, black womxn are not allowed to be fragile. We are normally the driving forces in our homes, even though a lot of the time, we make the least amount of money and get the least amount of respect. We are often the trendsetters in style, lingo, AND body type, yet equally just as invisible or brushed off as 'ghetto' while our white counterparts are celebrated for the appropriated content. We are everything...And nothing. Everyone sustains themselves from the metaphorical well that is 'Black Womxn Strength' – and as a black womxn, you are immediately cannibalized if you dare let that well run dry.

---

27 https://www.ncbi.nlm.nih.gov/pmc/articles/PMC1913079/

'As fat womxn and fat, black womxn, we should be able to be afforded the same luxury as our white counterparts, and be offered help, patience and support as, and when we need it.'

So, we are left with the suppressing choices of being a 'cautionary tale', or a shining 'role model' of morality. None of these choices allow us to experience the full range of living in our truth...which should include the right to be fragile and, at times, genuinely *not* okay.

In a perfect world, fragility stemming from eating disorders would be met with compassion and empathy, and it would be if I (and other plus-size black womxn like myself) were 'fragile', white girls. People, as well as medical professionals, would attempt to hold space for us and what could potentially be a cry for help. But no. If it's not us as black womxn being seen as 'strong' and therefore not needing or being reliant on help, then it's us doing 'what is best for our fat bodies in order to fit in with the rest of society', regardless of the consequences in both our minds and our bodies. As fat womxn and fat, black womxn, we should be able to be afforded the same luxury as our white counterparts, and be offered help, patience and support as, and when we need it. We cannot – as a society – continue to have a healthcare service that bases its diagnoses and optional duties of care on assumptions about bodies rooted in racial microaggressions and fatphobia, at the expense of disadvantaged people – it's killing us, literally.

Experiences of suffering from ED/mental health due to weight

'I noticed I had an eating disorder when I was 22 years old. This was after frequent hospitalizations for body dysmorphia and depression, two things I actually struggled with since I was much younger: around six years old. However, I had dealt with binge-eating disorder since I was around the same age. I would often hide after being bullied at school or by a family member for my weight, and just binge on anything I could find. My uncle once picked me up from gymnastics class to go to Burger King with the rest of my classmates and said: "Do you really think you should be eating that? Didn't you see the girls in your class and don't you wanna look like them?" From that day forward, I developed a serious restriction problem. I would unsuccessfully restrict only to binge later on.

By the time I was 22 and officially three years into an eating disorder diagnosis, I was weighing myself obsessively and developed a restricting habit from Weight Watchers. I do think there is a lack of visibility with plus-sized womxn as it pertains to ED because we're often not humanized. Eating disorders are often reserved, in conversation and psychological discourse, for perceptibly "docile", "socially attractive" womxn. The assumption is always that a plus-sized person, womxn especially, could not be suffering from an ED because she is not slim and only slim people are able to suffer. Considering it is plus-sized womxn that face the brunt of body-shaming, and have historically, you'd think that people would be understanding that this is very real for us. Because our

suffering does not look like visible collarbones and/ or visible slenderness, we are not suffering in the eyes of society. We are shamed, and ultimately, we are still blamed for the shame we receive. "If you don't want to be fat, get over it and stop eating," I already have. I already exercise multiple times of day. Those were my responses, but they could not see the deep issue and the self-hatred because they thought that as a fat black girl/womxn, I was supposed to just change.'
– Chantal (@ChantalJS13)

'I would force myself to vomit after meals or not eat all day or skip meals. Especially after any meal I thought was fattening. I did tell my family but since I was eating and also was black my family was like that's not a "thing" for us. I got some treatment from my therapist who treated me for other issues. There is no actual visibility. There was none then and not any now. Most people feel if you're plus-size, how can you be struggling with food? But it runs so much deeper than that.'
– Anon

'I first recognized my behaviour as an ED right as I was entering treatment. It started at the end of high school. I've always been fat, since at least pre-school and my parents and grandparents are fat and I started dieting with them when I was seven or eight but I just kept growing (like I was supposed to, LOL) and also kept getting fatter. Before high school was over I'd lost about 50 lbs (26.5 kg) and that summer between high school and college I lost 30 lbs (13.5 kg) more. The disordered behaviours started pretty soon after I started losing weight. First, it was just fasting the day of the weigh in and then I started binging after the weigh-ins and then after a while the binges went from one meal to the whole day and then to a couple days until I was binging half the week and then starving myself the other half leading up to the weigh-in. This was the summer before college and I was desperate to lose as much weight as possible so I started using laxatives and diuretic pills to help lose weight as well and ultimatelyI started purging. I didn't do it all the time, a couple of days a week and this went on for five to six years with some breaks in

between. *I didn't tell anyone until I started ED treatment. I knew all the while that I was doing this that it was fucked up and I hid it. There's a definite lack of visibility because people feel sorry for people with eating disorders and think of them as poor emaciated little girls but they instinctively hate fat people and blame them and their fat for everything that's wrong with them and they can't reconcile those two things.'*
– **Anon**

Clearly, the issues surrounding fatness and mental health, as well as eating disorders is an issue that needs to start taking centre stage not only in the interests of fairness and diversity, but for the sake of the many plus-size people who have gone through, and are still going through it. To provide more context from a professional point of view, I had a chat with my mate, Natasha Devon (MBE – put some respect on her name!), who is a writer, speaker, and campaigner/activist for mental health and body image issues, and who also recently launched the **Mental Health Media Charter** – a UK-based organisation which is committed to discussing and reporting stories relating to mental health in a safe, helpful, and responsible manner.

Natasha Devon MBE on mental health and weight

Me: *'In your opinion, why do you think society as a whole is so reluctant to – I guess – incorporate some of the blame or responsibility when it comes to contributing to the negative mental health of fat people?'*

Natasha: *'People have been relentlessly misinformed about health for decades with an over-simplified narrative of "personal responsibility". Most people still see a person's weight as a direct and sole consequence of their diet and exercise habits, which they in turn view as questions of "willpower" and "discipline". We are also consistently told that being healthy is inextricably linked with morality.*

Many people therefore see fatness as a defect of character and something the individual unquestionably has the power to change. There's a massive divide in the public consciousness between this and characteristics the individual can't change – like race, sexuality, or height – when it comes to how socially acceptable it is to show prejudice.

This in itself is deeply problematic. Even if all the above assumptions were correct, and people were fat solely because they sat on their arses eating lard all day, why should that mean they shouldn't be afforded the basic care, respect, and consideration which are essential to mental health?

Add into the mix the "tough love" philosophy advocated by "gobs on sticks" in the media (and which holds that if we "really" cared about fat people, we'd shout at them until they were too ashamed to eat, out of concern for their "health") and what you have are multiple factors which conspire to create a consistently hostile culture for fat people. It even bleeds into the practice of some medical professionals, who have been shown in numerous studies to take less care with fat patients. Yet because most people don't know there are more than 100 unique contributory factors which determine a person's weight and that fat stigma actually encourages less healthy food and exercise habits long term, they simply retort "well, do something about it, then".'

Me: 'What do you think schools, institutions, or the media can do to help younger plus-size people cope with the pressures of body image?'

Natasha: 'Young people need to be exposed to a diverse range of bodies. There's no point in giving them a one-off lesson on the perils of photoshop in the year, in an attempt to combat 364 days of constant Kardashian-style white noise. The human brain is constantly drinking in information and subconsciously laying down belief systems which affect how we perceive and interact with the world. We also learn through repetition – that's why we are all, to a lesser or greater extent, a product of our environment – our environment is responsible for the things we hear and see repetitiously. That's why I created lesson plans for schools aiming to get young people to diversify their social media feeds – it's important they don't just see people who look and sound like them in their online wallpaper.

I also think plus-size teachers and parents can play a role, particularly with young children. If they are constantly belittling their bodies, children will pick up on, and emulate this. Conversely, if they respect and celebrate their bodies, children will have positive role models. Of course, that can be hard when they might be receiving a barrage of negativity and microaggressions from the people around them, so we all have a role to play.'

Me: 'Have you ever noticed a difference in how different cultural groups deal with mental health and body image?'

Natasha: 'I'm from a mixed-race family so I'm related to West African, Jewish, and English people. I'd say on average the black womxn in my family have much better body image than the white womxn. Two of my black aunties in particular are huge in every sense (tall and fat), carry themselves like Queens and dress themselves without apology. This was super inspiring for me growing up (hence my enthusiasm for children being exposed to diversity), but now I'm older I recognize their attitude must have been the result of a lot of previous struggle for acceptance.

On the other hand, the views of my black family are more regressive when it comes to mental health. It's still largely seen as a sign of "weakness". This is backed up by UK national statistics – BAME people are statistically more vulnerable to severe mental illnesses like schizophrenia, particularly if they are first generation immigrants. Since mental health issues exist on a spectrum, it's reasonable to assume there were symptoms of depression and anxiety which preceded the development of psychosis, but they were not addressed. This isn't all down to cultural attitudes (access to services and discrimination are also relevant) but it's certainly a factor.'

Me: 'What would you say are the most common mental health disorders associated with weight/fatness?'

Natasha: 'Eating disorders are the obvious answer here, but not in the way you might expect. Everyone assumes the only ED which related to fatness is binge eating disorder, but in fact starvation and purging mess up your metabolism, which can lead to weight gain, long term. Also, contrary to popular belief, the body is adept at "holding on" to most of what we consume, regardless of the measures we might take to rid ourselves of calories. Consequently, most people with bulimia are at the higher end of the "normal" BMI range (whatever that means) or overweight. Depression and stress are also associated with weight fluctuation – both are linked to an imbalance of cortisol, which overrides the body's natural hunger signals. Consequently, people experiencing depression or extreme stress will often either not eat, or eat in response to emotional, rather than physical cues. Depression also hugely reduces the motivation to exercise (which is why it's ironic that exercise is one of the best-known treatments for mild to moderate depression).

That's what a psychologist focussing purely on the Individual would say. As a campaigner, though, I also need to consider that the chain of causation operates in the other direction. Fat people are treated less empathetically by society, meaning the five key psychological needs (love, belonging, purpose, achievement, and being heard) are less likely to be met. Any marginalized group is statistically more vulnerable to mental health issues – in young people we see higher rates of mental ill health in first generation immigrants, children with learning differences, and those who are LGBTQ+. So, it makes total sense that the same logic would apply to fat people, who face a lot of the same prejudices and "othering".'

Me: 'It's known that people of all shapes and sizes can suffer from eating disorders, however society/ the media only seem to highlight those who have the physical/visible signs of it. Because of this, there are vast scores of undetected eating disorders found in men and womxn who are plus-size (I used to suffer from it too!). Do you think it's important for ED charities and the media to report on these disorders equally across the board, as opposed to just using – let's be honest – slim, white womxn as the poster child for ED?'

Natasha: *'First of all, black and mixed-race people experiencing anorexia often fly under the radar because they are genetically predisposed to higher muscle density, meaning that even if they are visibly underweight, they don't meet the BMI threshold for diagnosis. The whole idea that you can measure a mental illness via BMI is ludicrous anyway and something my friend Hope Virgo is hoping to change with her brilliant campaign "Dump the Scales".*

That's a side issue, though, because as you quite rightly point out, not everyone with an eating disorder is thin. There is an archetype which is actually an acknowledged part of the pathology of anorexia – Alice in Wonderland – a young, innocent, blonde, thin white girl who "falls down the rabbit hole of madness". (If you want to see this archetype brilliantly torn apart, read Kelsey Osgood's book, How to Disappear Completely*).*

Where people with diagnoses of other mental illnesses are often wrongly seen as violent, dangerous, and a burden on society, eating disorders are the ones which generally evoke sympathy – but only if they're the "right" kind. It has to be anorexia (because bulimia and binge eating are 'gross') and it has to happen in the body of a young, white girl to inspire public sympathy.

This is a poor reflection on society for a number of reasons:

1   *Because it tells us we're less capable of showing compassion to non-white people and men.*

2   *Whilst eating disorders generally provoke a reaction of "aaaah", they are also seen as something which exclusively happens to 'silly little girls' (because whilst young, white girls are considered aesthetically pleasing, they're also not taken particularly seriously).*

Changing the public perception on eating disorders is just one link in the gargantuan chain of sea-changes required to challenge a more broadly racist and fatphobic culture.'

How To Be a Thin OR Body Positive Ally

Do **you** have fat friends?

Are **you** the smallest one in your friendship group?

Do **you** constantly bang on about how 'fat' you are in front of your plus-size friend(s), or talk negatively about weight and dieting?

Do **you** talk about your food intake, and speak of 'good' foods and 'naughty' foods...in front of your fat friends?

Do you **often** bring up the weights and body shapes of celebrities and influencers in front of said friend?

If you answered yes to any of the above and you have ever spoken negatively of health, food or body shapes in front of them, you may just be an ignorant and inconsiderate friend who may be impacting negatively on your fat friend's mental health!

Never fear! I have a couple of tips below that may help you on your way to salvaging these missteps, as well as helping you be a lot more considerate of your friends' feelings when in their company.

1 Possibly one of the easiest ones to start with: **don't say 'fat' like it's a bad thing.** Don't tell fat womxn they 'aren't' fat if that is how they choose to describe themselves. Why? Being fat isn't a bad thing and shouldn't be considered as such. By saying 'you aren't fat', you're low-key telling them that being fat is bad and undesirable, and that you also don't see them as 'one of those fat people'. We are a broad and beautiful category with many multitudes. Don't tell me that I'm not a part of this group of people just because you like me and hate fat people. That's what we're NOT gonna do.

2 **Please for the love of Lizzo, DO NOT assume that someone has lost weight just because they look great.** 'You look so amazing in this photo! Did you lose weight?' No Sue, I haven't lost weight. I just look great. One doesn't need to have lost weight in order to be seen as attractive. I can be fat and exactly the same size as I have been, and still look like a snack. Let's let these toxic behaviours rest.

3 **Talk about something aside from appearances. For once. Please. PLS.**
In the UK, we live in one of the most image-obsessed places in the world, but sometimes, I seldom have a casual conversation with another smaller womxn in which their fad diets don't come up. I remember when I used to work full-time in a variety of different jobs and lunches with my colleagues were always fraught with concern about everybody's various dietary restrictions and anxieties. It's so common for womxn to shit on their own appearances. Self-hatred is so ingrained in most womxn that they don't know where they'd be without it and are fearful or resentful at the idea of giving it up, and I just don't think that people who hate themselves could be good allies to someone else.

This Fat Body Has Been Complicit In Breaking My Brain!

'Please DO NOT assume that someone has lost weight just because they look great.'

4 **Don't act all surprised when we show up looking cute AF.** You have to be careful with your tone, especially when you're giving a compliment on a style or an outfit. A lot of the time, it can come across as a pity compliment – or a sense of surprise when you see that my outfit looks cute as hell. In my opinion, I feel it's always better to say 'that outfit looks great on you!' instead of 'you look great in that!'. The difference is very subtle, but it makes me feel like I put LIFE into the item (which of course I did because DUH!) as opposed to the piece giving ME life.

5 **Don't assume we are all on diets.** My least favourite phrase is 'are you sure you want to order that?/are you sure you can eat all of that?' Am I sure I want to order this 12-chicken nugget meal with a Mcflurry on the side? Why yes, Margaret – I'm pretty sure I do, OTHERWISE I WOULDN'T HAVE ORDERED IT, WOULD I?

6 **Please understand the impact and weight of your words.** One of the most annoying things to go through as a fat person is to hear friends or loved ones talk about how huge or fat they are – when they are in my presence and I am clearly the larger person there. We have been learning to love and accept ourselves, and to let the outside reflect the inside. It's something that is incredibly annoying, because there is always the implication that they are ugly or disgusting for having the extra weight. It always stings and sometimes you can end up internalising it, even if they are completely oblivious to what they are saying.

7 If you're someone who benefits from slim privilege, **quit speaking on behalf of, or over fat people, and start speaking in support of, and with fat people.** Look I get it. You're trying to be a good thin ally in a bid to stand in solidarity with the fats. You tweet the self-righteous tweets. You make the IG stories talking about how 'society needs to be more responsible on the subjects of fat-shaming and inclusivity' and you take a photo of yourself hunched over so your followers can see that you too, suffer from 'fat' yet are STILL a normal person. *Wunderbar*. Great! But the vast majority of the time, what you do not realize is that these acts of allyship comes across as extremely self-serving. What you're doing is that, instead of using your privilege to uplift and highlight minority/fat voices, you're centring yourself within the conversation and making it all about your perspectives and opinions – as well as your body type.

8 Don't get me wrong – it's GREAT if you've decided to help your fellow fat pals by talking about fat acceptance! **But before you type or speak – ask yourself if you are talking about the movement in the *right way*.** If you're claiming it for yourself as something you get to rant and rave about, then you're not really pushing a paradigm shift around fat acceptance. All you're doing is making yourself look compassionate and smart, building off of the hard work of people more marginalized than yourself. And that's oppressive.

9 **Speak up when someone body-shames your friend.** If you think that your friend would be comfortable with you speaking up, be ready to defend them when trolls or just horrible people IRL emerge from under their bridges. At most, it can help your fat friend become more assertive in defending their own beautiful bodies (or, if they choose to not engage, to perhaps use self-care to help prevent themselves from internalising the hateful words). At the very least, it'll show your friends that their feelings and body are valid and worthy to you. When someone is being an arsehole, just knowing that you have an ally who respects and supports you can do wonders for your mental health.

10 **Listen when they need to vent about their bodies.** It's important not to try and silence your friends when they bash their bodies. Rather, it'll be better to try and help them reframe certain attitudes that seem to be causing them personal strife, and let them cry over the difficulties of self-love, which can be incredibly tough sometimes. Between things such as racism, colourism, and fatphobia, maintaining a semblance of body positivity can be EXHAUSTING at times. It's okay to let your friend release this stress without making them feel guilty for their negatively charged words.

Coping with mental health when you're from an ethnic minority

First off, let's acknowledge that dealing with any kind of 'new age', mental health-related, non-Christian related issue is always going to be tough in general when you come from an ethnic background. I think a lot of non-white households are rooted in tradition, with faith and spirituality being the pillars by which they hold their standards to. I'm from a Ghanaian family where things such as mental health aren't openly discussed as such so it's always going to be a bit tricky to navigate! Here's how I navigated my way through:

Recognition and patience. It's difficult, but sometimes you have to recognize that our parents are from a completely different generation and culture than us, especially for those of us who are first or second generation immigrants. And so seemingly 'progressive' things such as mental health illnesses are still rather new for them. For the longest time, they've been told to pray bad feelings away, so for us to go up to them and tell them that our brains are broken? It's...it'll be a new concept. In that instance, it's okay to be patient.

Education. I mean, one can only be patient for so long before you need to talk, right? If you can (and only if you can – don't try and force it if your parents don't seem the type to listen – I get it!), try and sit your parents down when they are in a good mood, and explain to them how you feel. Let them know that you are feeling extremely vulnerable (don't use the word sensitive – in my experience, parents can wield that word around like a weapon) and that you'd like for them to just listen for the time being while you explain. While explaining, try and feed in some education about the illnesses, be it anxiety, depression, or whichever condition you identify with.

If all else fails, journal. Look, sometimes it's not going to go well. I get that. If you find that your family are resistant to listening to you, don't try and put pressure on them. Just leave it and start journalling your thoughts and feelings. Even if you have someone outside your immediate family you can chat to, it's always important to have YOUR safe space too.

Find a therapist. You can find a race/ethnicity specific therapist if you wanted to also, as that can make things a lot easier when you have the familiarity present.

Understand that there's nothing wrong with YOU.
The gaslighting can be real sometimes, so regardless of what they say, just know that there is absolutely nothing wrong with you. You are deserving of support, and you are also deserving of the same basic humanity. Remember, your mental health matters!

Chapter SEVEN

Hyperpigmentation?

It Must Be The FAT

Replying to @StephanieYeboah
But you still got **weight** issues. Enough of PC, you are fat and likely to get **health** problems. Medical fact. So shut up and sit down, 200 times.

Replying to @StephanieYeboah
I mean you're just at a higher risk for a heart attack, a stroke, type 2 diabetes, sleep apnea, high cholesterol, high blood pressure, fatty liver disease, gall bladder disease and cancer.

Replying to @StephanieYeboah
The word isn't Fat though it is Obese. Fat is the slur of Obese. The diagnosis of somebody who is dangerously overweight with health problems is Obese. You can be an Endomorph and not be classed as obese but rather healthy if to be measured up on the BMI scale.

just a small percentage of the health-concerned trolling I receive on Twitter. Lovely, innit?

Before I get into this VERY, VERY FUN chapter, I would like to point out the following things in order to make the health trolls mad:

'Fatness is not the opposite of health'

'Fatness is not the opposite of health'

'Fatness is not the opposite of health'

'Fatness is not the opposite of health'

'Fatness is not the opposite of health'

'Fatness is not the opposite of health'

<u>FATNESS IS NOT THE OPPOSITE OF HEALTH</u>

exhales Now that we've gotten that out of the way and hopefully scared off the trolls, we can continue. I was a bit wary about including a chapter on health, partly because it's been absolutely done to death, and there isn't anything different I feel I could add to the conversation that hasn't already been said by my amazing peers such as Megan Crabbe (@bodyposipanda) and Sofie Hagen. But...!! It's something that is almost a point of contention when it comes to being plus-size, and if we're being honest, we can't really have a conversation about weight without including health, because people are annoying and will always bring it up.

This chapter will be anecdotal for the most part, because I think it's important for you guys to see how fatphobic the healthcare industry in Westernized countries can be towards plus-size people; from using the word 'obesity' for fatness unnecessarily, to the ridiculousness of BMI, and the increase in online health trolling. I decided to open up my DM's to some amazing fat womxn who felt up to sharing their stories of the fatphobia they experienced at the hands of medical physicians and the healthcare industry. Before we get into that though, let's chat a bit about obesity, but also let's chat a bit about me and my relationship with health, because it's my book, innit?

'Bruise on your thigh?
OBESITY!'

With the exception of my inherited asthma and my fibroids, I've always been pretty healthy. Regardless of my size. I barely visited the doctor as a child, and would always freak out whenever I had the smallest cold headache, because ill health was never a part of my narrative. Before I continue, this isn't me trying to give myself a pat on the back for being 'healthy while fat' – even if I were unhealthy, I would still deserve the same amount of care and respect from society that everybody else is capable of receiving.

At school, while I wasn't the most active child, I wasn't sedentary either. I used to play football on the boys' team (BECAUSE GOD FORBID SIR JAMES BARRIE PRIMARY SCHOOL WOULD CREATE A GIRLS' TEAM. THE HORROR #FEMINISM). I participated in after-school dance classes in secondary school (to the sheer amusement of my school mates because as you know, it's hilarious to see fat people moving rapidly, if it's good for their 'health'). Despite all this, I would still hear calls for me to lose weight from the school nurses, and anytime I would go for my asthma check-up, I would be asked to lose weight. Like clockwork. Every time. Even as a child, I was incredibly confused as to why all of these adults wanted me to lose weight. I felt fine. Aside from the asthma-induced wheeziness, I never felt out of breath or heavy, so what was the big fucking deal?

As you guys already know, I was bullied pretty badly in school. On one occasion, I was in chemistry class and we were in the middle of doing a practical lesson where we had to handle some corrosive liquids. Unfortunately, I was also taking the class with a couple of the boys who used to bully me and, in this specific class, they thought it would be absolutely hilarious if they squirted the back of my neck with some of this acid. Which they did. I just remember a section of the class erupting into laughter, with the science teacher completely unaware, as I ran to the nearest sink to wash the stinging liquid off. It wasn't lethal liquid, but I do remember the back of my neck feeling raw for a few days after.

Over the next few months, the back of my neck began to darken quite considerably, taking on an almost leathery, flaky texture. Upon going to the doctor to complain about this sudden hyperpigmentation, I was told that my weight was the cause of the darkness around my neck, otherwise known as Acanthosis Nigricans, and if you're a fellow plus-size gal who also suffers from hyperpigmentation, you may have heard this condition thrown at you a few times too.

Acanthosis Nigricans in a condition that is thought to affect plus-size people more than non-plus-size people, and it is the name for dry, dark patches of skin around the back of the neck, groin area, armpit area or anywhere else around the body. A lot of the time, it is a sign of an underlying health condition – predominantly diabetes, an underactive thyroid, or PCOS. The actual condition can be harmless, or can appear due to simply just being fat, or being black.

'Society likes to insult and judge fat people for being fat, with suggestions of us going to the gym or losing weight "for our health", but the gag is that they actually want us to stay fat otherwise they will have no one to feel superior to.'

Despite me telling my doctor that I had been scarred by this corrosive material, they took one look at me and decided that MY FATNESS was the cause of the burns on my neck. MY FATNESS GUYS. Notwithstanding the fact that I normally suffer from hyperpigmentation on other areas of my body such as between my thighs (chub rub), my cleavage, and the side of my body, it was my FAT that FORCED the melanin to congregate around certain areas of my body.

Honestly, if I had a pound for every time a faux medical online troll found a pic of my body online and would scream, 'SHE HAS ACANTHOSIS NIGRICANS BECAUSE SHE'S FAT, WHICH MEANS SHE WILL DEFINITELY GET DIABETES!!!!' onto a gossip message board, I would be a very rich womxn! Because I am someone who rarely gets ill, I've always made it a habit to get myself checked out whenever I can. This includes blood work such as my blood pressure and sugar levels, as well as general upkeep. I have never had high or low blood pressure, and my blood sugar levels have always been excellent. So, you can take your ACANTHOSIS NIGRICANS and shove it up your anonymous arses because it doesn't give you a right to body-shame me or anyone else, even if I DID have it.

Obesity is such a dirty word, isn't it?

Look, I'm not stupid. The vast majority of fat people – both online and IRL – aren't stupid. We are well aware that being bigger can carry a risk of certain diseases.

We've been told that our hearts will spontaneously combust by the time we reach 40. We've been told that we ABSOLUTELY WILL get heart disease and diabetes. We have had people wishing for our deaths in order to be 'proved right' for years and years. We get it. Hey, hey...

Honestly.

We get it.

Despite the plethora of other (admittedly) choice-led activities that can lead to a detriment in health such as smoking, drinking, and drug use, which one is the 'most' demonized out of them all? Which ones are continuously glamourized within the media? That's right.

Smoking, drinking, and taking drugs. Rock and roll! Elegant! Classy! Rebellious! Fun! Sophisticated! Cool! Suave! All adjectives associated with these highly addictive and dangerous pastimes in the media and in society. Yet, walk around in your size 24 jumpsuit eating a protein bar and suddenly the pitchforks come out and you are accosted with unsolicited comments about how you're going to die when you're 30 (I'm proud to say that even while writing this in my 30th year, I trekked up two!!! mountains in two!! different countries that year and my heart is still kicking, thanks for the concern though Darren) and that you 'would look a LOT better and a LOT healthier if you slimmed down a little' (thanks @SmallPeen84 on Twitter).

One of the easiest ways people use health as a way to fat-shame is by using the word 'obesity' in the first place. Obesity. It's such a gross word, isn't it. It's a word loaded with so much hatred and prejudice. Let's first see how obesity is defined in the dictionary:

'Obesity: The state of being grossly fat or overweight.'

I find it interesting that the healthcare industry and society only choose to use medical terminology when it comes to fatness. If someone is 'grossly slim', what are they called? Remember, anorexia is a mental health issue so that wouldn't be the appropriate word. What about if someone is taller than normal? Are they always referred to using a special medical term? What about muscular people? Lean people? Any specific medical words to describe their bodies? No? Oh, okay so it's just the fatties that are dehumanized – gotcha.

There are two types of reasons why I think it's a horrible word: one a bit scientific, and one more ethical.

The scientific reasons to get rid of the term 'obesity' applies to anyone with a BMI (which...LMAO we'll come to that FACADE of a measurement later) of 30 or higher. But why does medicine and public health use this term then? Well, the main idea is that if you are 'obese', you are in a medically deficient state that apparently needs addressing. In particular, you are at increased risk of developing things such as type 2 diabetes, heart disease, some cancers, orthopedic problems, sleep apnea, and some reproductive problems, among other things. Some of these conditions are potentially life-threatening, so losing weight and becoming smaller is a compelling health goal. That's the story anyway.

But is it true? No, not as stated above. Not all BMI numbers 30 and above are created equal. In a widely-cited study which took place in 2013[28], Katherine Flegal and her co-authors found that people with BMIs 30–35 did not have a higher risk of death than people with BMIs in the 18.5–24 range. Higher risks of death were documented in BMI ranges above 35. And lower risks of death were documented for those in the 'overweight' range of 25–29.

Flegal's results have even been duplicated and extended to show that obesity just isn't a useful word to refer to a medical condition. In an article[29], Ann Barnes cites data taken from the United States that shows that weight affects life expectancy differently in white womxn and black womxn – for black womxn, weight isn't a risk factor until a BMI of 40 is reached, vs a BMI of 30 for white womxn.

There is so much more data out there showing that obesity isn't one category at all – it's a range of different categories that apply differently to groups depending on age, race, ethnicity, gender, income, geographic location, etc. A one-size name simply doesn't fit all.

Let's now turn to the ethical reasons behind the word. I found an amazing article during my research written by Dr Stacy Carter[30] in 2013, who brilliantly said the following:

> 'In this... social and political sense, obesity is associated with powerful negatives, stemming from both long-standing prejudice and recent public health framing. These include epidemic threat, devastating impending costs, tragedy (particularly children routinely dying before their parents),

---

28 https://www.ncbi.nlm.nih.gov/pubmed/23280227
29 https://www.ncbi.nlm.nih.gov/pmc/articles/PMC4473617/
30 https://newsatjama.jama.com/2013/02/14/jama-forum-separating-the-science-and-politics-of-obesity/

as well as poor character in obese individuals, who are frequently implied to be lazy, to lack willpower, to be greedy, or to shirk personal responsibility. This view is used to legitimize the well-documented discrimination experienced by heavier people, especially womxn, particularly younger womxn and girls. For people above normal weight, then, public discussion of obesity is fraught.

Obesity in the sociopolitical sense also became institutionalized fairly rapidly in universities and governments in the late 20th century. There are now obesity strategies, government departments responsible for obesity, obesity handbooks, professorial chairs, university research centers, websites, Twitter feeds, and advocacy groups with the word obesity in their titles. So obesity as an amorphous but potent social and political concept now raises the stakes in many settings, engendering blame, inducing strong feelings, and providing the focus for many people's professional roles and identities.'

In short, shouting 'obesity!!!!' in a crowded doctor's office raises alarms, brings on waves of shame, provokes stern and dire warnings about DEATH, DIABETES, and HYPERPIGMENTATION, and puts everyone on notice: Something. Must. Be. Done. Now. But maybe nothing needs to be done??? Or maybe something does need to be done, but what that is will vary loads, depending on a bunch of complex factors. It's not a uniform call to lose weight, come what may.

I know, we can't solve these issues just by getting rid of the words. But getting rid of them would be a step towards acknowledging that the story about weight, health, and illness is a very complex one, and using 'obese/obesity' confuses us, misleads us, shames us, and blames us. So, let's get rid of it. When we need to talk about people's weight, there are lots of other words around—let's use them instead, I think. Also, maybe let's not always use weight as the main factor in every, single thing. It's tired, and boring, and old, and prejudiced. Especially when you factor in the nonsense that is BMI.

BMI (Body Mass Index) – quick reasons why it's shit!

Body Mass Index is a unit of measurement that gives you a 'score' depending on your height and weight. You are in the 'normal' weight range if your BMI is between 18.5 and 25, overweight if it is between 25 and 30. Anybody with a BMI of 30 or more is obese. OOoOo.

What I find funny is that every couple of months or so, we have these huge medical reports[31] that condemn BMI as being utterly flawed (with proof!), but then somehow society tends to forget all about it and carry on as if it's a respected, current unit of measurement. Guys. BMI is NOT an accurate measurement of health at all. STOP IT.

'But why, Steph? YYYY?' I hear you ask. Well, let's spill some tea:

* It was a unit of measurement that was created by a statistician, NOT a physician.
* It was designed for populations, not individuals.
* The formula was created based on the average white man (so LMAO?!)
* The formula was altered to fit the data.
* It doesn't take into account bone or muscle mass.
* The formula measures physical appearance, NOT health.
* The formula also doesn't take into account race, sexuality, and overall body composition.
* My mum is 5 foot exactly and wears a UK size 8. She's TINY. According to her BMI, she is 'obese'. I HAD TO LAUGH.

---

31 https://www.nature.com/articles/ijo200887

Reasons your 'concern for our health' isn't helping anyone. At all

'I'm JuSt cONcErNEd AbOUt THeiR HeAlTh.'

'I'm body-positive, but I don't believe in GLORIFYING obesity.'

'I think fat people deserve respect, but I think they also really need to focus on their health.'

'Studies have shown that obesity is the second leading cause of preventable death, so I can't support that lifestyle.'

Shut up. Stop. Just hush pls and let's talk about why this behaviour is so incredibly toxic.

1 **Because fat-shaming makes you look like an arsehole.** Let's just come out and say it: If you're a 'concern' troll, you're a fat-shamer. And if you're a fat-shamer, you're being mean for no reason whatsoever. You may have the best intentions, but what you're really doing is kicking people when society is already holding them down. Like bitch, we know society hates us. Do you really need to rub salt into the wound? Enough already.

Concern-trolling does not make you a hero. You're not saving anyone's life.

You're not motivating anyone toward health. You're not helping someone cope with oppression. You're hurting people. All concern-trolling does is hurt people – both individually and socially. And if that isn't a good enough reason to re-evaluate your actions, then what is?

2 **You're contributing to the 'Bootstraps' myth.**
Popular belief would have you convinced that being
fat – like living in poverty – is a choice. And if you
just *work hard enough* to pull yourself out of your
desperate situation, then you too, can enjoy the
privilege brought on by being thin! But just like
we don't have much choice about our economic
status, we don't have much choice about our body
types either. And while we can *try* to change both,
we will probably encounter more obstacles than
opportunities. So, when we perpetuate the narrative
that we all have a choice in whether our bodies are
fat or thin, we push the idea that everyone should
be striving toward thinness all the time – and that
is something that actually harms us all.

In the meantime, we also push along the
notion that since fat is unhealthy and therefore
bad, the 'choices' we make about our bodies also
speak to our moralities and the extent to which
we 'deserve' good health and respect.

Instead, we should recognize that none of
us has control over the hand we're dealt in life, and
that we're all deserving of respect, REGARDLESS.

3 **Because mental health is still health.** I'm pretty
sure no one's health has ever been improved by being
ridiculed. In fact, I'm pretty sure there's research to
back up exactly the opposite. Because when you take
the piss out of someone, or a group of people, based
on their social disadvantages, especially when you
hold the power, it's called *bullying*.

And beyond the social problem of fatphobia,
there's also the individual, one-on-one kind, where
people take their socially-constructed, anti-fat bias
and actively use it to tear down another person's
self-esteem.

This can take the shape of tossing slurs toward
a fat person who's out for a jog. It might be whispers
and giggles in response to someone walking down
the halls at school. It might be hanging up pictures
of people you see as unattractive in their fatness to
serve as your 'thinspiration'. Ugh.

Or it might take the shape of leaving comments on fat-positive threads, pounding into the ears and eyes of everyone who comes across them with the same old bullshit rhetoric being spoken by the public at large, tbh.

But mental health is just as important as physical health. And if you're really, truly concerned about someone's well-being, it matters to not deteriorate their emotional and spiritual health, doesn't it?

At this point in what will probably turn out to be a short chapter, I could go into a rant about how people shouldn't judge others' health based on weight. How trolls and fat-shamers use our health as a way to insult our appearances without coming across as dickheads, and perhaps go on to defend our right to live and thrive as human beings without the constant policing of our bodies. What I'm going to do instead, is to pass the mic over to you guys. The next few pages highlight your stories and your experiences. There were so many of you who were keen to tell your stories about the way in which you've been treated by doctors.

So many of you spoke out about being plus-size, and being plus-size womxn of colour, who have faced prejudice in some way, or have been told that your weight was an issue for a complaint that had absolutely nothing to do with your bodies. It's important that your stories, our stories are heard, and for the medical industry to finally take heed and listen to our stories, instead of potentially putting our lives in danger based on your prejudice.

'I miscarried at 11 weeks when I was at uni and in the follow-up appointment with my GP, she asked me if I'd considered losing weight and referred me to an aerobics class. Like three days after the pregnancy failed. As though clearly all that garlic bread had killed our child.' – **Anon**

'My most recent incident was a womxn at Planned Parenthood who told me that I definitely had PCOS without doing a single test (I don't) and then said I would definitely get cancer if I didn't lose weight because of the PCOS that she assumed I had. I was furious and actually ended up verbally fighting this womxn while I was stark naked.' – **Anon**

'I have type I diabetes and have had it since I was seven. This is different than type II and is not associated with weight. My psychiatrist (NOT my endocrinologist) suggested during a check-in for mental health meds that I look into gastric bypass to cure my diabetes. It took explaining to him THREE TIMES that I don't have that kind of diabetes and weight has nothing to do with it.' – **Anon**

'I used to have chronic tonsilitis when I was a teenager, and every time I went to the doctor to sort it out I was told I needed to lose weight. Since I got my tonsils out they've moved onto talking about my weight when I come in for an ear infection.' – **Anon**

'I was having back issues after a really bad fall where my back was basically slammed into the sharp edge of a stair on a bus. They told me to lose weight. Currently trying to get someone to diagnose me regarding issues with irregular periods after coming off of birth control. Everyone immediately goes to PCOS and say lose weight, but nothing about my testing indicates I have PCOS.' – **Anon**

'I went to the doctor for an armpit swelling, and she told me that "she could barely see it" and that "sometimes fat just shifts around." Went to get an ultrasound and the (lovely, fat) technician was like "whoa yah look at this swelling, let's find out the cause." She was the only one who acknowledged the swelling was abnormal – I went to four (thin) doctors. In the end it was tendinitis.' – Anon

'I was plus-size and pregnant – I went to the maternity assessment unit as I was in a lot of pain at 32 weeks the doctor came to scan my baby and could see a lot of fluid but instead of investigating the cause he sent me home and said I was just a "big girl having a big baby and that's what happens the heavier you are the more you hurt". Two weeks later my baby passed away of a cardiac tumour.' – Anon

'In my mid-20s, I went for my yearly check-up to the pulmonologist regarding my asthma. After telling me that I had the lung volume of a swimmer and that I only needed asthma spray during an allergic reaction, he asked me how much I weighed. I told him my weight and he pulled out a very old looking chart and said that my BMI was too high and if I had thought about weight-loss surgery. For reference – I was a UK 22/24 at the time and the doctor had just said that my lung volume and function was better than good.' – Anon

'My fave was when I went was told that the reason I had a huge blind spot and flashing lights in my eye was because I didn't exercise enough. At the time I was going to the gym every day and also in the middle of a severe bulimic episode. Turns out I had optic neuritis, and the second doctor I saw confirmed it had absolutely nothing to do with my weight. Classic!' – Anon

'I physically lost my voice for a month and the doctor refused medication and said that if I lost weight there wouldn't be as much pressure on my throat and that way I wouldn't get strep throat.' (Author note: WTF?!) – Anon

'I went to the rheumatologist about pain management for fibromyalgia, a condition which I've had for six years now – her verbatim words were "you don't need pain management, you need bariatric surgery and a can-do attitude." Literally will remember that with shame and anxiety for the rest of my life.' – Anon

'I've been dealing with a knee injury for the past four years. I know it's an injury, because I did it while dancing. I haven't had insurance to get it checked out. I finally did this year. After telling her all of my symptoms my doctor did an X-Ray and told me it was arthritis and I just needed to lose weight. She prescribed me ibuprofen and sent me on my way. About two months ago my knee has gotten worse and it's very unstable, so now I'm in the process of switching my insurance so that I can get a second opinion. I'd also like to add that I informed her of my anxiety and depression. She also attributed that to me being overweight and would give me a recommendation to a therapist. Instead I was only sent emails about nutrition classes.' – Anon

'Went to the GI doctor, as I had been having horrible stomach pains, nausea, etc that just wouldn't go away. As soon as the doctor walks in, he goes "I know what your problem is. You need to lose weight." Made him do some tests and turns out I have a chronic stomach condition.' – Anon

'I went to my GP to complain about lower stomach/abdo pains and not having my period for a few months. I really don't know where my weight could come into play but was told losing weight could help make my period regular and I'm most likely suffering from period cramps. That was their solution. No more than a week later I started my period (so I thought). I went to A&E because the pain was getting too much to bare and I was actually pregnant and having a miscarriage.' – Anon

'I was told by my GP just a week ago that I couldn't have HRT because of my weight. He's wrong; I did my own research through menopause specialists and there are HRT options for me. I'm in despair about this. After a decade of struggling to get adequate mental health care, I'm now facing a fight to get menopause treatment. I'm completely flattened.' – **Anon**

I decided to leave the longest anecdote till last. Read it. Absorb it. These are some of the lengths the healthcare industry go to when ignoring our pains and placing the blame on our weight.

'My mum fell ill quite suddenly and drastically with confusion and a fever; an ambulance was called and paramedics suggested that she likely had an infection and should see her GP. We took her to the GP who after very little testing, deduced that she had a urine infection; she was prescribed tablets, told to drink water and rest. The next day, we found my mother paralysed in bed, unable to move. She was rushed to A&E where they then preemptively diagnosed that that the infection had probably progressed too far and she had developed sepsis; she was put on antibiotics and remained virtually unconscious for three days. She eventually regained some consciousness, enough to tell us that her stomach hurt. Doctors told us that this was probably due to her being unable to eat and the heavy medication she was on, despite me telling them that her stomach looked noticeably swollen and that she had reported stomach pain. I'm sure doctors didn't really pay any attention to this comment because a fat stomach inherently looks "swollen" in comparison to a thin stomach. After four days in hospital, we were told my mother could go home despite her not being able to eat, stand up, or even urinate unaided. I pleaded with doctors and had to explain to them that my mother, up until a few days prior, was a working womxn (the director of her own business) and that there is no way she was recovered – she couldn't even stand up or remember what day it was! The doctor told me – and I quote – that he had assumed she was normally "vegetative" based on her weight *(this is problematic for a number of reasons, but the notion of assuming my mother's fat not only rendered her immobile, but also meant she had limited cognitive brain function is sickening). I pleaded with more nurses and they were sympathetic and worked to get her some more tests. They scanned her stomach with a small device; it looked fine. The first proper full body scan they did of her stomach revealed she had a perforated stomach ulcer; her stomach had effectively exploded due to an ulcer which is what caused her infection and sepsis. She was rushed in for emergency surgery, which she came through with the support of every single piece of life support equipment available but died 24 hours afterwards. The stress of the ineffective treatment and previous misdiagnosis meant she did not stand a chance of recovering from such major surgery. What continues to haunt me is that "morbid obesity" is listed as one of the causes of her death on her death certificate; not misdiagnosis, not the fact that scanning machines aren't effective on fat bodies, not the fact I had to plead with doctors to get them to give her tests (what happens to fat people in hospitals who are alone, without advocates? I often lie awake at night wondering this). Now she's dead, her public record reads that her fat was the reason she got ill and died – and I have to live with that as a fat womxn myself today.'* – **Anon**

The healthcare industry clearly has a long way to go when it comes to the process of destigmatising, as well as humanising fatness. Granted, no one is saying that being fat is a walk in the park for some people, but it doesn't give these healthcare professionals the right to gloss over potentially life-threatening diseases and illnesses by using our weight as a one-stop-shop diagnosis. Fatphobia is growing like bacteria cultures in a petri dish within our healthcare system, and it **needs** to change.

I am more than my weight. And I need and deserve to be taken seriously. PERIOD.

'Fatphobia is growing like bacteria cultures in a petri dish within our healthcare system, and it needs to change.'

Chapter EIGHT

The Lizzo Effect, Otherwise Known As 'ABOUT FUCKING TIME'

RINGS KLAXON Hear ye! Hear ye!

All hail MELISSA VIVIANE JEFFERSON, also known as Lizzo, First of her Name. Grammy-nominated (at the time of writing), *VOGUE* cover girl, owner of number-one singles and multiple fashion cover spreads. The Twerking Flautist. We SEE YOU.

And can I just say...about time. About. Bloody. Time.

I decided to name this chapter after Lizzo because of what she represents. Not just diversity within music, but representation. Representation for me and so many other fat, black womxn who thought they would never see themselves on screen. Lemme just...let's just start at the beginning.

A wild fat appears on America's Next Top Model

Bitch, I have watched every single episode and every season (bar the last four, TBH) of *America's Next Top Model*. I was in love with the fashion, with the sheer dramatics of it all, but mostly, I was in LOVE with 'The Walk'. One of the judges of the show – Jay Alexander – became my muse. My idol. As the catwalk coach of the show, I adored how graceful he was as he floated down the catwalk. How feline-esque he presented himself to be. How the clothes just melted into his skin as he pranced. I wanted to be him. I too, wanted to be delicate.

I also wanted to stomp the runway and feel that air of confidence as if nothing could get in my way. I remember practising my catwalk nearly every day and always hoping that one day, they'd cast a fat girl in the show. Even just a little fat, she could even be a size 14 or so. I just wanted to see a STOMP on that runway for crying out loud! Just a little morsel of excess fat so I could get the visibility I so desperately needed.

Then my girl, Toccara, came along for the third season. A stunning, gorgeous, tall, black, plus-size womxn who was there to represent for the big girls. I. FELT. SEEN. Even though she eventually ended up in seventh place (she was ROBBED I tell ya), I felt like finally, the TV Gods had heard my call. Was this about to be the start of something amazing? Were plus-size fat girls finally about to get our dues on TV? Were we going to finally have fat actresses who DIDN'T just play maids and Mammies? I placed so much faith in Toccara – almost like she was Moses or some shit – that she would lead the fat, brown womxn of the world into GLORY, and that it would finally be our time, our time right now, to shine!

I remember during the season that she was on TV, I started taking up dance classes in school. I started taking drama a lot more seriously, I started violin lessons, took choir, and I even auditioned for weekend stage school. I wasn't accepted, which still kills me to this DAY because I gave the performance of a lifetime with 'Killing Me Softly' by Dionne Warwick (as sung by The Fugees, obvs). There was something about having that small window of opportunity on TV for womxn that looked like me, that gave me some kind of hope. I too wanted to sing and dance and strut my stuff in beautiful gowns. I wanted to act and play instruments and just see how far I could go creatively. It was one of the rare times in my early teenhood where the hope felt ever so real. For those couple of months, I too felt like I could be, and achieve anything. That was until she was booted off the show.

Toccara later appeared in a spread in Italian *Vogue* and earned some bit-parts in some American TV sitcoms but after that, she seemed to fade away, as did my dreams for having that representation. I was absolutely gutted for her, but also for me. Would we ever get the representation we deserve? Would we ever have our fat Beyoncé? Would there ever be a fat, black womxn on the cover of a magazine? *exasperated sigh*

'Who...who is this FAT ANGEL ON MY INSTAGRAM?!'

It must have been around mid-2017 that I became aware of the force that is Lizzo, although she had been on her grind, doing music on the underground scene for much longer than that. I was on Instagram as per usual, browsing the page of one of my favourite fat-centric accounts (@ashleighchubbybunny – FOLLOW HER FOR AWESOME FAT CONTENT) and I came across a photo of Lizzo in some kind of black Lycra outfit and I instantly fell in love.

I remember over the course of that week I must have liked every single one of her photos. There was something about her that just screamed confidence: she was fun, she was honest, she had oodles of talent, and her style was off the charts. I just knew that following her would have a profound effect on me, SHE was the content I desperately needed to see on the big screen, and so we, as her fans, all waited and supported her with bated breath in anticipation of her big break.

Cut to 2019, and Lizzo is everywhere. Her breakout single 'Juice' was being played on every radio station. The AMAZING video was being shown on TV. She was being flown out to perform on late night TV shows, festivals, and award shows, and her gigs were selling out by the minute. Being able to watch all this as a spectator was wondrous to behold. Before this, myself and other black, plus-size writers were growing increasingly impatient and frustrated with the amount of non-inclusive campaigns that were being continuously shipped out in the name of 'body positivity'. I was getting so tired of constantly seeing mediocre, hourglass-shaped, white womxn be seen as 'brave' and 'so strong!' for doing the bare minimum when it came to the movement. I was sick of seeing the same privileged bodies being cast as the 'body positive icons' in a movement that they ripped from under our feet.

Looking at Lizzo's Instagram feed and seeing her slow rise to the mainstream inspired me. I couldn't believe that in my lifetime, I was witnessing something that I never thought would ever happen – ever. For the fat community, and more specifically, the fat, black community, Lizzo not only represents a megaforce of talent in the spotlight making a name for herself, she also represents the antithesis to the 'Mammy' stereotype often cast on fat, black womxn along with the matriarchal-yet-subservient demeanor that accompanies it.

Suddenly, the feelings that were around during my *America's Next Top Model* phase began to flicker once more. Here was an unapologetic fat, black womxn at the top of the charts, living her best life, and slaying the game. Designers were creating outfits for her. She was killing EVERY photoshoot, and she was getting the recognition, respect, and visibility she deserved. It felt like I was looking at the version of myself I could be, and it made me feel somewhat...invincible?

I remember being invited to an intimate gig of hers one evening and I couldn't believe how excited and happy I was to go. It felt like I was going to see the Spice Girls for the first time, but in this instance, she was THEE fat Spice Girl. Someone that I could actually look up to in real time and feel inspired. I watched her, tears spilling out of my eyes as I mimed along to her electrifying set. She was giving me Madonna circa the 'Vogue' years, in this pinstriped suit complete with corset. I was gagging for it okay?! It wasn't until her set finished, that I realized that I had been crying the entire way through, and that I was a bit of a blubbering mess on the dancefloor. It was at this point that a member of her record label noticed me in tears in the crowd and asked if I wanted to come backstage after the set.

GUYS, I COULD HAVE JUST SUNK INTO THE FLOOR AT THAT POINT.

Me? Little old me? A snivelling fan, embarrassing herself in the middle of the dancefloor, to meet the amazingness that was Lizzo? I couldn't believe it! As I was led backstage, I could feel my heart doing knots. Due to the severe lack of representation and visibility growing up, I'd never had what one would call 'an idol' or at least, someone to look up to. But now it seemed to be happening at ultra-fast speed and my heart could barely take it.

208

We entered the room and there was Lizzo, looking like an absolute vision. She stood up and gave me a hug, after which I burst into tears while she gave me the biggest cuddle. The snivelling mess I was, told her that she was an incredible inspiration to not only me, but the thousands of people who look like us, and that she was the type of person I needed to see growing up, and would I have had that content, I would have probably grown up feeling a lot more valuable and loved as a human being. She also started crying while consoling me, telling me that she was doing this for all the plus-size, black womxn who felt they didn't have a voice and, in that moment, I felt so whole. I felt that this may be the start of something huge, not just for Lizzo, but for black, plus-size womxn like myself.

One question, however, burns in the hearts and minds of those living in fatter bodies: does the acceptance of a figure like Lizzo equate to acceptance of those who possess the same demeanor AND body that she does? Are we as a society really ready to accept that fat, black womxn are more sexy than they are 'brave'? Are we ready to accept that fat, black womxn have always seen themselves as great and talented, yet it has been the weight stigma glazed in white supremacy that has inhibited our ability to excel? What happens when the 'Lizzos' of the world are not making music and entertaining the masses? What is to be said about the 'Lizzos' that are your neighbours and family members? OK, that was quite a few questions there, but you catch my drift.

While those of us who are fat are not expected to have confidence at all, listening to the opening of 'Truth Hurts', Lizzo makes her declaration extremely clear, 'I just took a DNA test, turns out I'm 100% that bitch'. Twerking on stage while playing the flute (!!!) with skill and finesse, Lizzo exudes such beautiful confidence with a surety of her body's abilities. She is not reminiscent of the fat, black Mammy whose main purpose in life was to be the caretaker of others. Neither is she the depiction of the sassy, fat, black womxn who is full of strife, using deception to get what she, in society's eyes, could not otherwise qualify for. Quickly, Lizzo dispels any idea that what she does is a minstrel of sorts. Rather, she puts on a show similar to that of her smaller counterparts, obliterating the myths steeped in weight stigma that one cannot be fat and active, or fat and skillful, or fat and confident. Furthermore, Lizzo has no problem sharing the stage with other fat, black dancers, reinforcing the premise that we are a community of many, and she is absolutely not alone.

In the book, *Fearing the Fat Body: The Origins of Fatphobia*, written by Sabrina Strings, Strings lays out another way in which white supremacy was weaponized against larger, black bodies to offset its desirability and morality. Strings argues, based on her research, that throughout the 19th century, fat, black bodies were framed to be immoral due to the alleged excessive amounts of food they inherently needed to consume. How can eating food ever be immoral? FOOD IS LIFE. The shenaniganry[32] of it all. Coupling this with the already derogatory beliefs about black people, the

---

32 I'm SO happy that I've finally been able to use this in a sentence!

church encouraged restraint among its white members, leaving black people who possessed larger bodies and practiced Christianity to internalize the stigma placed on them. Furthermore, this also made it okay to attach other negative attributes to existing while being fat (i.e., laziness, gluttony, etc.), ultimately framing weight stigma as we know it today.

As Strings, and others who preach fat liberation point out, the stigma associated with weight isn't about health. Rather, it's a tool for those in power to wield, with the assumption that if utilized properly, their status within our society's hierarchy will remain intact. Therefore, the goal of weight stigma has always been to keep people who live in larger bodies abased, shamed, and regretful for what *they* have allowed. It's to see their identities as 'spoiled', wasted, and only redeemable through the attainment of a smaller body. Lizzo spits in the face of this system, and I for one, am living for it.

Seemingly enough, there's a certain naivety to think that because Lizzo's music is climbing the charts, being played on the radio, and is accepted into the homes of millions of listeners around the world, somehow those who look like her will be as well. And that's the gag right there. That with the beautiful tune of the 'Truth Hurts' chorus, families will start to see fat bodies as great, able, and valuable. However, ironically enough, with the acceptance of an 'other', it feels like the UK, the US and...well, most Western countries have this weird thing where they whitewash your identity to be simply 'human', something the mainstream can easily digest.

For black celebrities anyway, with fame comes the caution to not become too 'political'. Just ask Colin Kaepernick and Mo'Nique. This isn't a new phenomenon. History shows us that speaking up for the lives of others deemed unworthy has cost celebrities their careers. Ultimately, the goal in silencing what some define as 'identity politics', is so that those who are marginalized will not use their platform to raise awareness and create social change. In Lizzo's case, she's currently making an amazing stand against weight stigma, however, the song topping the charts, making her most visible, is left open to interpretation by the listeners as to who that '100% that bitch' can be. So, it's easy to listen to 'Truth Hurts' and never hear Lizzo's 'truth'. It is easy to accept the message, while simultaneously discarding or whitewashing the messenger. So, where does this leave fat, black womxn in the long run? Interpersonally? Changed? Lizzo is the representation some of us have been waiting for! She is the self-confident friend/auntie figure who egged us on to dance in the kitchen. She is the fashion forward cousin who encouraged us to wear that crop top and booty shorts. She is the best friend who reminded us of our worth when a fuckboy stopped calling. She is our queen that inspires us to liberation in the face of a system that is hellbent on reminding us that we don't belong. Systematically? We're still trying to see where this leaves us. The quest to fight weight stigma is a long and hard one, often taking victims along the way.

What can be encouraged is that Lizzo's message not be whitewashed or undersold for the masses. She is an exceptionally talented artist who has had to face weight stigma, coupled with racism (and still does) relentlessly on her way to fame. She has a story that should be told, accompanying her music. Listeners should try to put her lyrics into context to understand her as an artist and learn more about the world fat, black entertainers live in. Because it's going to take more than a fat, black womxn topping the charts to eliminate weight stigma, even against herself. Many will love to listen to Lizzo's music and despise her body all the same, and that's the tea.

Lizzo is an anomaly within the music industry, walking in the footsteps of the Jennifer Holidays, Missy Elliotts, and Martha Washes (The Weather Girls). She is a light to the fat community. A treasure to those that understand that you can't separate the personal from the political when you live within the margins of society. May she continue to give us music that uplifts our spirits, while giving us interviews that stir us to question our assumptions of body acceptability in society!

Where are we now?

I've spoken here and there about situations in my personal life which have related to the topics I've covered in the book – albeit in a non-chronological order – so I guess that leaves us with the here and now. What am I up to? Where am I, on this spectrum of fat liberation and self-love? What have I been doing over the past few years to get me to where I am now?

Well! Today I can say that I am a (somewhat) successful freelance multi-hyphenated creative; a plus-size style/lifestyle influencer, freelance writer, public speaker, sometimes broadcaster, AND NOW PUBLISHED AUTHOR, FFS I cannot believe?!

Did I think that my life would end up this way? Absolutely not. Had I listened to my dad, I would currently be an extremely depressed lawyer with a severe lack of lust for life. Had I not gone to Barcelona – where I finally realized that weightloss wasn't the be-all-and-end-all – or New York, where I gained the inspiration to start a fashion blog, I could bet I would probably still be choc-full of low self-esteem, bad decisions, virtually no confidence. Every decision – bad or good – I've made, has led me to where I am today and not only do I feel much more enlightened in regards to speaking out about body politics and social justice issues, but I finally, for the first time in life, recognize and understand my worth.

I spent a large amount of my early blog days shouting and screaming about equality within the plus-size industry: not just with the types of bodies that were constantly on show, but the races and abilities of those on show. Throughout the years, whilst even facing backlash from some of my peers as well as blacklisting from some huge brands, I remained steadfast and continued to fight my corner. Not only because I wanted better for myself, but I wanted better for all the plus-size womxn who looked like me. For those who don't have the 'preferred' hourglass shape or white/light skin. For those whose FUPAs are the stars of the show. For those who have big arms and no butt (*points to self*), for those who want to see their beauty reflected back at them. For those who need acceptance.

Today, I continue to campaign against weight stigma in the media and beyond, alongside waxing lyrical on topics such as mental health, self-esteem, plus-size fashion, and confidence. A large part of what I do wouldn't have been made possible without the amazing fat community that I find myself to be a part of – especially online. I know it may be a bit premature to say, but I honestly feel that a change may be coming.

With the rise of some incredibly talented plus-size, black womxn who are trailblazing in their respective industries, both in the UK and the US, it just feels like finally...FINALLY, we are beginning to get the recognition that we have so desperately craved.

We have reached nowhere near the amount of visibility we deserve, especially within the media, but this rise in amazing black, plus-size womxn within the fields of modelling, literature (Hey Candice! Author of multi-award-winning bestselling book, *Queenie*), advertising, and performance art, demonstrates that we are actually slaying DOWN right now, and I for one, am absolutely loving to see it. Let's celebrate these womxn. Uplift them and show them that they matter. Our thoughts matter. Our perspectives matter. Our opinions matter. Our autonomy matters. Our bodies matter and are capable of being beautiful too.

I decided to have a chat with Vanessa Russell, Sophia Tassew, and Enam Asiama, three plus-size, black womxn who are currently making strides within the worlds of fashion and advertising, and who I am also proud to call my friends. We talked about the industry, Lizzo's impact, trials and tribulations, and what we can hope for the future for plus-size, black womxn, in their own words.

Vanessa Russell, 26

Vanessa Russell is a Curve model, mental health, and a creative, who has modelled for, and appeared in campaigns for brands such as ASOS, Simply Be, Lazy Oaf, and Universal Standard, and has appeared on the runway at London Fashion Week. A true fashion babe!

Vanessa: *'I have been a signed model for three years and honestly the word struggle would be an understatement! Being black and plus-size in this industry isn't the easiest – it's not all doom and gloom but it's neither a bed of roses. There are some really challenging days and some days full of hope and opportunities. On days that are not so nice, I am lucky to have a solid circle of amazingly strong and encouraging womxn who just get it. To be a model, you have to have a strong sense of self and resilience is a must, otherwise you will not survive this industry.*

I can't think of another job where you are constantly being judged and valued by your identity. I am a black Curve model with locs and I'm guessing a lot of clients see my hair as an inconvenience. Sometimes I joke and say that me being black is their limit, me having locs is pushing it!

It's sad because I sometimes sense that my white counterparts feel as though when these issues are discussed, it's just me moaning because after all we all struggle but I don't think white models are faced with these challenges.

I am also half of a creative collective called CTRL V+E. It was a combination of the challenges me and my friends faced in the industry looking the way we do, coupled with not having any creative control, as well as the influences of people such as Lizzo who exists unapologetically as her fat self in the spotlight, that encouraged me to start a creative collective with one of my best friends, fellow plus-size supermodel and now creative partner, Enam Asiama.

Our existence in the industry alone is a political statement because our image and identity go against traditional standards. We are here to STAY.'

Enam Asiama, 25

Enam Asiama is a creative, public speaker, influencer, and plus-size model, who has a background in events management, and has starred in campaigns for brands such as Selfridges, Universal Standard, *Refinery 29*, Target Beauty, Paco Rabanne, Maison Margiela, and Sephora. We love high fashion!

Enam: *'Being plus-size and black in this industry to me is still a one-of-a-kind experience. I am a super-fat womxn and being in this body – even within the plus-size, black community – is still considered a unique body type. Even among my friends. I don't consider my body type to be the ideal, even within the body positive space. There still isn't a lot of plus-size, black representation out there, so I definitely think that I'm setting the benchmark for what we can achieve, especially within high fashion.*

High fashion is so different to commercial fashion. I feel somewhat powerful when doing commercial shoots as I still feel like I have a voice and can say when I like something and when I don't. With high fashion, however, it's almost like you're made to feel grateful for being there, as your body type has been "specially chosen" to represent a specific demographic. I've suffered a great deal of struggle in the modelling industry. With being black, fat, and queer, you suffer the most violence because people have their preconcieved ideas of you and misconstrue how you present yourself, as there's still this idea of how fat womxn should be seen. Everything we do has to be 10 times the effort of a smaller model, as well as having to strive for greatness and equally not be "too loud". Microaggressions can be a real issue too within the industry, normally from cisgendered white people.

There is so much tokenism within the industry, and as much as I love Lizzo, I do feel like she has been tokenised by the entertainment industry. It's almost like she's the new poster girl for a new "Fat Beyoncé". Even though she's been working hard and going through hurdles, people can't seem to put her in her own lane – she still has to be compared to another celebrity.

I do love the fact that she's creating her own rules and speaking out about body positivity and acceptance – it feels like a reflection of me.

I think for years and years, we've always had plus-size womxn in the entertainment industry; from your Jennifer Hollidays to your Mo'Niques, Jill Scotts, and Octavia Spencers of the world. It's been the influence of this "influencer culture" that I think has inspired brands to capitalize on this movement, simply because we have been able to create our own platforms to tell our stories. I think that's why people such as Lizzo can thrive in this day and age. In turn, we've also been able to capitalize and monetize off our passions and the things we care about as plus-size black womxn, as well as being able to tell our stories.

Things that can be changed within the fashion industry from my experience, is how they view the opinions of fat womxn. They should be able to trust that we know how to dress ourselves, but also know that they are dealing with a fat womxn, so they should have our sizes ready on set. A lot of the time, I've had to wear my own clothing on set because the brands and casting agencies are never prepared.

It's also important for brands to think of fat womxn as competent, fashion-forward womxn who also like to dress well, and would like the option to wear the same pieces as our straight counterparts. When you offer us plain black, misshapen pieces, it shows that you do not care about us.

If I could go back and talk to a 15-year-old Enam. I would tell her not to change a damn thing, because everything that I have done thus far has led me to where I am now. I'm finally at a point where I am beginning to see visibility and representation for myself and others, and that's such a beautiful thing. I'm so fortunate that I was rebellious and stubborn to those around me who told me to lose weight or make myself smaller for the comfort of others. I would tell her that she is so "badass" and fucking cool, and that she will figure it out as she gets older. The world hasn't shown her kindness and may never will, so it's okay to have your own back, as that's all you have. I'd tell her to keep striving, as there's no one out there like you. You are THAT bitch.'

Sophia Tassew, 23

Sophia Tassew is a plus-size model, brand ambassador, author, and advertising creative/art director.

Sophia: *'Being plus-size and black is many things. It's my identity. It's the first thing people see before getting to know me as a person and because of that, I feel that I have a duty to ensure that we are moving in the right direction. Sometimes I don't want to have to wake up and think "what's going to happen next?" or think about what part of my humanity and identity do I have to defend this week? I have to be really hyperaware of myself. I'm blessed to be in the body that I'm in but at the same time, it's not as freeing as people may think it may be.*

With Lizzo being on mainstream TV and on virtually every fashion cover that has come out over the last year or so, I think it's amazing for her and the people who resonate and see themselves in her, especially identity-wise. Online, however, it seems to be a different story. I see a lot more hate than I do love towards her which is really upsetting to see. I feel let down, especially by some of the black community in this instance who I've seen a lot of the hate come from. With Lizzo being on all these platforms though, I definitely think it's a step in the right direction though. She's not a typical size 16–18, so it's always going to be a bit of a shock I think to the audience, but it's definitely something that is needed in this current climate. She makes me feel validated, and I think she makes a lot of people feel like that. Equally though, I don't know what that'll mean for other fat, black womxn who want to make it in the industry in terms of progress, because there's still a lot of pushback towards her, for reasons that I don't think make any sense whatsoever. I know the hate isn't anything to do with her music or anything – it's more to do with the way she looks and so I think society has a long way to go in accepting and lifting up fat womxn, and fat, black womxn.'

Mirroring the musings in my earlier chapter about fat womxn in the media industry, while we have made massive improvements over the last couple of years in regards to visibility, we can agree that so much more can be done within the fields of entertainment, advertising, literature, and the creative fields. Sophia, Vanessa and Enam make up just a tiny percentage of the amazing plus-size, black talent that is emerging from the UK at the moment. Talent such as:

Giselle Ali: Giselle is a celebrity makeup artist whose focus is on black skin and beauty specifically. Giselle travels all over the world, in particular Western Africa, to create the most amazing aesthetics, and her clients include Cynthia Erivo, Munroe Bergdorf, SZA, Nadia Rose, and Adwoa Aboah. Giselle has been featured in publications such as *Who What Wear* and *Elle Magazine*. We stan an international beauty babe!

Queen MoJo: I came across the amazing Queen MoJo online sometime last year via Trina's Curve Catwalk account and I have been absolutely obsessed ever since! Queen MoJo is a motivational speaker, talk-show host, online personality, self-love and mental health advocate and plus-size influencer and advocate, as well as an incredible dancer who has featured in music videos, and her quick wit and hilarious social media skits bring me so much joy! She inspires me to put myself out there more and dance to my heart's content, because we look amazing doing it!

Trina Nicole: Trina is one half of award-winning natural hair and empowerment influencer duo, CurltureUK. Not only does Trina slay the game with her beautiful locs and curls, all the while providing tips and tricks on how to best maintain and love our hair, but she is also a content creator in her own right, a plus-size model, and a dancer, who has danced not only at Glastonbury with none other than Lizzo herself, but has been in some incredible adverts throwing shapes and letting the world know what she's made of. Trina is also the founder of The Curve Catwalk, a London-based size inclusive dance class for plus-size womxn – the first of its kind in the UK.

Not to mention stunning, plus-size models such as Olivia Campbell, Simone Charles, and Lauren Nicole, award-winning sex positivity blogger Shakira Scott, actress Lolly Adefope, and...well...little old me doing bits and bobs, I suppose!

Lizzo is just the start and we absolutely cannot deny the impact she has had for a lot of plus-size young womxn today, including myself. She's paved the way for the millennials and Gen-Zs to start acknowledging our worth. She is the catalyst to providing hopefully more fairness and inclusivity within the entertainment AND fashion industry. She is the first plus-size womxn on the front of *Vogue*.

VOGUE.

As in. Do you know how monumental that is? History has been made. Fashion designers are very slowly beginning to extend their sizes. There is still some progress to be made where the sizing is concerned, but I'm seeing a lot more UK size 22s and 24s than I used to – which is to say – I've never seen them before, so the progress is there, in small increments.

We've had plus-size love scenes, plus-size villains, plus-size stand-up comedians, and plus-size underwear models.

We've gone from us playing Mammies and slaves, to selling out concerts, books, and winning awards. We've gone from being seen as a monolith based on sadness, laziness, depression, aggressiveness, and 'undesirability' to being seen as dynamic, multi-faceted people who can demonstrate strength as well as vulnerability. Who can be happy and fat! Who can stand up for ourselves! Who can exist happily within different intersections, while trying to positively carve a space out for ourselves to prosper! Who can sing, and dance, and educate, and love (and be loved in return!), make money, be accessible, have families, be successful, and can be happy! Basically, we are just like everyone else, and we deserve the same love, care, attention, respect, and basic humanity that the rest of society are afforded.

My hope for the future is that – not to get all Martin Luther King on ya – one day we can all just co-exist together without the fat-shaming and bullying, without the policing of our bodies, and without judgement and trolling. But let's face it, asking for all of that is like asking any member of the Kardashian family (bar Kourtney) to start dating white men – it's just never gonna happen. Not to mention the other things we as a society still have to put up with: racism, colourism, classism, all-the-other-isms, homophobia, transphobia, *patriarchy*. But hey, it's a start, eh?

It's incredible that it's taken this long for our voices to be heard by society at large. Body positivity – for all its faults – has catapulted us to the mainstream. It's given us a portal by which to share our stories with the world, to give people an insight as to how we see society, and a look into how society views us. It's given writers like myself the opportunity to share the injustices that fat womxn, black, fat womxn, and fat womxn of colour have had to face in society. It's given us the tools to educate those who would otherwise 'other' and marginalize us. All of us, the influencers, the activists, the writers, the advertising executives, the models, the stylish, fat womxn popping into Greggs on her lunch break, the vibrant, fat womxn eating alone at a restaurant, the beautiful fat couple at the movie theatre having a blast, the fat person writing a beautiful piece of poetry for their university project – every one of us right now are setting an example. We are changing the game. WE are the stories. WE are the reference points. In 15+ years, people are going to look back and Google image our pictures, read our articles and books, look at our campaign photos, and watch our videos and think, 'This is it. The 2000s was one of the turning points within fat liberation'. We'll be the ones being studied in schools and name-checked in dissertations. ISN'T THAT WILD?

Most of all, the fat community has allowed us to lift each other up. To process trauma in a safe environment. To educate each other. To celebrate our fat bodies. Our magnificent, massive arms. Bodacious, Buddha bellies, terrific, tree trunk legs, big, beautiful boat feet, chipper chub rub, stunning stretch marks, our Rubenesque rolls. It's given us a space to learn how to love ourselves loudly and unapologetically in a world that wishes to silence us and make us small.

Well, we aren't small. We're fat bitches, we deserve to be here. We are beautiful. We deserve to reclaim the very word used to harass and hurt us, and we aren't going anywhere anytime soon.
MIC DROP

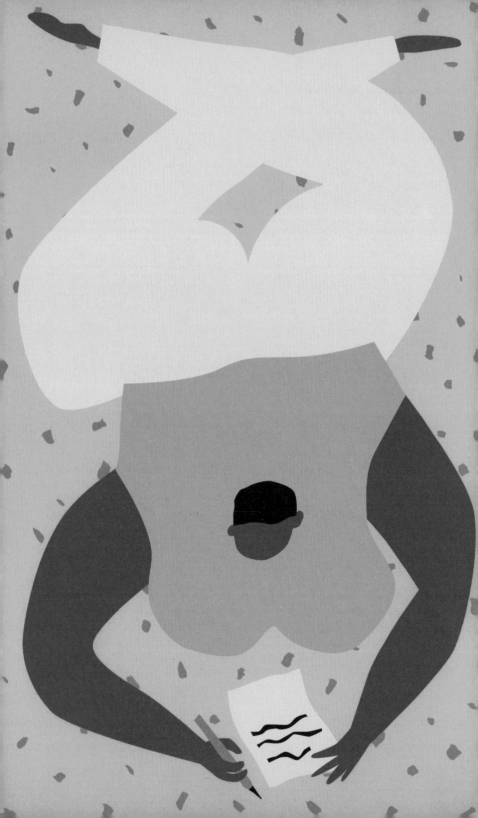

Chapter NINE

Dear Body...
I'm Sorry

One of the most popular questions I get asked from my
readers and followers is, '*How did you get started on your
journey to self-love? What are some things you can do?*'
    I tend to give a variety of responses, such as looking
in the mirror and finding something beautiful about yourself,
buying cute underwear, surrounding yourself with a positive
community, etc, but the one thing that I always come back
to, that is a guaranteed GIVEN for me, is writing a letter
to your body. You can write it at the very beginning of
your journey, when you're halfway through, or when
you're just feeling down. I find it an extremely emotional
and powerful way of getting in touch with your body and
seeing your body for what it is objectively: your tool to life.
An object that helps your consciousness get around. You
have the opportunity in that moment, to see your body for
what it is and apologize to it. Congratulate it. Compliment
it. It's a trick that never fails for me, and whenever I'm
having a shit body day, I think about all the things my
body has done for me and I sit and meditate for a bit. I will
always advise people to try it. It doesn't have to be some
grand thesis, it can be some little hand scribbled note
with a paragraph, but as long as you speak from the
heart, that's THEE most important thing.
    It's incredibly important to change the way in which
we speak about our bodies. Words can have a huge impact
on our self-esteem, and constantly talking negatively about
our bodies can reinforce the idea that there is only one
type of body shape that is beautiful.

We have been brainwashed our entire lives to feed it nothing but hate and resentment, that sometimes, having to be nice to it seems like a bit of a chore. As well as writing letters of apologies to ourselves, there are so many amazing, proactive things we can do to show our bodies the care it so desperately requires. Things as simple as sleeping or taking naps to give your body time to rest, repair itself, and cleanse itself, eating good food that tantalize the senses, massages (either professional or done by a loved one), stroking yourself (and I don't mean in the sexual way ALTHOUGH THAT ALSO WORKS TOO) – our bodies are SO sensitive and responsive to not only the physical touch of others but also from ourselves. Next time you're lying on the sofa reading or watching TV, just stroke your own arm, or your belly, or your chest. I do it sometimes when I'm watching TV and I find it incredibly self-soothing and comforting, especially when I'm feeling low!

Other ways in which we can change the way we talk about ourselves include the following:

Taking the One Week Challenge

If you can, challenge yourself to a week of no negative body talk. It might be hard at first, but if you tell friends and family about it, they can support you and even try it for themselves and if they can't do it – choose not to be around them until that week is over.

Focus on Fun Talk!

Avoid negative body talk when discussing diet and exercise, focusing instead on the emotional and health benefits. So, if your friend or family member has started a new fitness regime, perhaps ask them whether they're feeling stronger or sleeping better, as opposed to the weight aspect of things. Why? Because weight doesn't matter.

Let your friends know you're not here for the constant body chats

Next time you meet up with a friend, if they start any fat talk or negative body chat, reassure them but also alert them to the negative impact of their words – for example, 'I adore you and it hurts me to hear you talk about yourself that way', or 'I'm sorry but I can't engage in this type of chat – it's not good for me'.

Stop being negative towards others' bodies (that includes celebs too!)

229

Stop making criticisms about other people's weight or looks, and that includes celebrities too! Sure, we all like a gossip, but we've seen what fatphobic gossip online looks like (just ask Lizzo). Just because you think you are far removed from the problem by not talking about yourself, it doesn't make the words any less impactful on yourself or others you talk to. Instead, try writing something nice about them instead!

Which leads us nicely into the next bit.

So, for you I present, the letter to myself. Perhaps at my most vulnerable, so strap in lads! Also, if you're reading this Mum...Sorry!

also be prepared for several trigger warnings including eating disorders and self-harm

Dear body,

OH BITCH WHERE DO WE EVEN BEGIN WITH YOU? Girl. Sis. We have gone THREW it over the past 31 years, haven't we? One hardly knows where to begin. I feel like we got on well during my early childhood, don'tcha think? We were active, you allowed me to play with the boys during football at lunchtime, and I'd always be the one scoring all the goals, remember? The boys haaaaated to see it, but we loved it!

I guess our relationship changed around puberty, as it does with everyone else. Although – I couldn't understand why my boobs grew and sank, as opposed to staying pert like the other girls. I didn't understand why you did that – why you just... decided to go south like that. That was the beginning of the resentment if I'm being honest. I hated the fact that you started to rebel against my wants and desires for what I wanted you to look like.

Secondary school, you took a bit of a battering. Not just from the kicks and punches of the bullies, but from me too. I started hurting you – a lot. I realize now that what I was doing, I was doing under my missguided interpretation 'self care'. I starved you constantly. I used scissors to cut into the faint stretchmarks you created on my round belly. But it's like...you didn't care? The more I starved you, the more I forced you to empty the contents of your stomach, the more I cut into you, the bigger you got. The rounder you became and the more I ached physically, mentally and emotionally. I used food as a way to abuse you; it felt amazing, yet empty at the same time, it's the only way to describe that period of my life.

We got older and yet you still kept chugging along, much to my contempt. At that point, I felt as if I'd thrown every single diet, detox and weight loss method at you, but STILL you wouldn't slim down. I bombarded you with laxatives and illegal diet pills in my early 20s, though. Remember that? You finally did my bidding, and got smaller, but at the cost of my mental health. I guess back then you were trying to tell me something, but me being ever the stubborn person, refused to listen.

But look. Eventually it clicked. Remember when you got really small and I just stared and stared at you for the longest time. I stared at your bruised, broken skin and it was then that I realized... what the FUCK.

No seriously. What...the fuck...was I doing this for? Who was I doing for? I'd spent my entire life trying to shrink myself for other people. I was apologising to people FOR you, instead of apologizing to you, for everything I'd put you though. I'd starved you for years. I abused you willingly. I called you ugly, disgusting, unlovable. I cut into you repeatedly in a bid to make you smaller. I filled you full of toxins and poisons. I called you useless. I abused you repeatedly. I said you could never amount to anything and used words with you that I would absolutely never say to anyone else. I blamed my lack of a romantic life on you and how big and ugly I thought you were. Sure, we had a nice year and a half of solace during my first and only relationship, where I felt really good about you because you were finally getting what you wanted and felt desirable for the first time in your life but when that ended...I went back to hating and blaming you, instead of blaming society's hatred of bodies that look like yours.

And for all the above, I am sorry.

I am so, so sorry.

Sorry for hurting you, sorry for abusing you and sorry for any harsh words used against you. I'm sorry for blaming you for all the feelings I didn't know how to carry. I'm sorry for believing others over believing you.

Throughout the last few years of accepting you, the one thing I haven't done is apologize for the way I have treated you. I wanted to change you. I tried to erase your beautiful melanin. I cut you. I harmed you. I tried to kill you. I didn't want you to be a part of me. I hated you.

I think back to my youth and think about how much you have gone through; you've been broken, bruised, bloodied, burned and pummelled but you did not once give up on me. You recovered; you healed. You're the reason I'm still here. Your resilience and strength is outstanding; how could I ever hate something that has fought to keep me alive for so long? I have finally reached the point where I love and accept you. Your stretch marks tell a long and complicated story, but a fascinating one nonetheless. Your marks and scars leave behind tales of strength and courage. Your saggy boobs will one day (hopefully) nourish your children and keep them strong. Your skin colour has been passed down to you from a nation of people known for their beauty, tenacity, grace and strength. You possess all the character, beauty, confidence, sass and sex appeal you could ever need. You are irresistible. You are amazing. You are strong. You are resilient.

You may not be what is categorized as 'beautiful' within what the mainstream find desirable, but fuck it. You are a bloody GAWDESS. You are beautiful, and I love you. You deserve love. You radiate love, and you deserve and are entitled to your happily (or: fattily – see how I linked it to the book?? MY MIND) ever after. You are perfect.

Much love, always,
Stephanie

Plus-Size Brands

234   Some of my favourite plus-size (and plus-size friendly) brands

I like to think that one of the many positives to come from the fat acceptance and body positivity movement was the emergence of more fat-friendly apparel; something that had been greatly missing from the (albeit online) Highstreet until now.

Fashion has always been integral to my identity and how I choose to present myself to the world, and as well intentioned as some of the old school brands may have been, I did not want to present myself through the medium of draping, shapeless smocks, open shoulder blouses, butterfly and quote motif print T-shirts and ill-fitting trousers (pants). Because at the end of the day, why should smaller bodies have all the fun? While there are still some ways to go in achieving affordable, inclusive fashion for all bodies, the brands opposite, are a good start if you're looking to cultivate a capsule collection, or just pick up a simple, statement piece.

It's worth noting that some of the brands listed are fast fashion brands. We still aren't at the point where the majority of mainstream and sustainable brands cater to fatter bodies, so until then, if we want fashionable, inexpensive clothes, the fast fashion route will continue to be an option.

Clothes

* ASOS Curve
* navabi
* River Island Plus
* New Look Curve
* Calvin Klein Plus
* Levis Plus
* PrettyLittleThing
* Missguided
* Glamorous Curve
* Daisy Street
* Neon Rose Store Plus
* Violeta by Mango
* Another Reason Curve
* Next
* Marks & Spencers
* Vero Moda
* Micha Lounge
* Pink Clove
* Lovedrobe
* Universal Standard
* Penningtons
* Chi Chi London
* Zelie for She
* 11.Honoré (for your plus-size designer bits!)

Lingerie

* Figleaves Curve
* Curvy Kate
* Playful Promises
* Scantilly by Curvy Kate
* Calvin Klein Plus
* Elomi
* Savage x Fenty
* Wolf & Whistle
* Tutti Rouge

Sportswear (that are available in plus-sizes)

* Nike
* adidas
* Puma
* ASOS 4505
* Yours Clothing
* Evans
* Fabletics
* Zalando

Acknowledgements

Seeing as the general topic of this book speaks to issues regarding self-love, where else to start but thank myself for being so aggressively awesome? Intelligence, humour, sass, wit – it's a full package really, so cheers, Steph.

Now that that's out of the way, let's get serious.

Always have to rep the most High and thank God for everything I do and for everything I've been through to get to this point.

I'd love to thank my commissioning editor, Kajal Mistry, and agent, Hattie Grunewald (and the team at The Blair Partnership), whose belief, trust, support and guidance in my work – as well as the ideologies I believe in – helped shape the framework of the book, as well as give me the confidence to actually finish writing it!

Thank you to the amazing design team at Evi-O Studio for bringing my vision to life with your stunning design and illustrations.

A special thank you to Michael Brooks, who made my face up and made me feel amazing while shooting the book cover on the day!

A huge thanks to everyone at Hardie Grant Books for believing in me, and for being so overwhelmingly enthusiastic and supportive of this project.

Thank you so much to my amazing managers, Gabriela Franchina and Harriet Driver, for their overwhelming and constant support and belief in me!

A *mahoooooosive* thank you to my photographer, Kaye Ford, riding alongside me on this epic influencer journey for the past three years. Thank you for understanding my creative vision and executing it flawlessly. Thank you for always telling me when I look crap, and for knowing my angles and making me so comfortable in front of the lens. I'm so happy that you came into my life and that we've been able to work together to create incredible content.

And finally, thank you to my family and friends, for all their continued love and support. Thanks especially to my family, who without them, I would not have the material needed to complete the anecdotal parts of the book. Cheers lads!

About Steph

Stephanie Yeboah has been a part of the fat acceptance/ body positive community since 2014, and since then, she has written many pieces on her blog, on social media platforms and in external publications on topics such as intersectionality in the body positivity movement, standards of beauty within the movement and self-love. This has led her to speak on panels surrounding these subjects at events such as the Women of the World Festival, Africa Utopia, the Youth Select Committee, the London College of Fashion diversity panel and many others.

'

Published in 2020 by Hardie Grant Books,
an imprint of Hardie Grant Publishing

Hardie Grant Books (London)
5th & 6th Floors
52–54 Southwark Street
London SE1 1UN

Hardie Grant Books (Melbourne)
Building 1, 658 Church Street
Richmond, Victoria 3121

hardiegrantbooks.com

British Library Cataloguing-in-Publication Data. A catalogue
record for this book is available from the British Library.

Fattily Ever After
ISBN: 978-178488-344-7

10 9 8 7 6 5 4 3 2 1

Publishing Director: Kate Pollard
Commissioning Editor: Kajal Mistry
Design and illustrations: Evi-O.Studio | Nicole Ho & Susan Le
Cover Photography and on pages 235, 236 and 239 © Kaye Ford
Copy Editor: Leanne Burbridge
Make-up Artist: Michael Brooks

Colour reproduction by p2d
Printed and bound in China by Leo Paper Products Ltd.